Dreams in the Life of Prayer

THE APPROACH OF EDGAR CAYCE

Dreams
in the Life of
Prayer

THE APPROACH OF EDGAR CAYCE

by Harmon Hartzell Bro

Harper & Row, Publishers

New York, Evanston, and London

1817

To Morton Blumenthal
    who undertook the first systematic study of Edgar Cayce's
    prayer states, from 1924 to 1933

CONTENTS

PART ONE

An Approach
to the Life of Prayer

CHAPTER 1

The Dreams
of a Musician

The dreamer is a man in his forties, a professional musician who both teaches music courses and conducts choral groups in a Midwestern university. He is a Quaker, married, the father of several children. Over a decade ago he underwent analysis in which dream study played an important part. Since then he has recorded and studied his dreams intermittently as part of his personal program for growth and self-integration. He includes in this program daily time for prayer and meditation, but when rehearsals squeeze it out of the daytime calendar, he occasionally tries to catch up in the middle of the night. From time to time he reads popular psychological works by Fromm, May, Frankl, Jung, and Tournier, and finds stimulus in introductions to Eastern thought by Watts and Heard. He has read many of the published materials about Edgar Cayce.

Asked to submit some dreams for the author's research project on dreams and prayer, he began with the following:

You ask first about dreams which have affected my prayer life by grounding my approach to God in a better awareness of His nature and presence.

I think of a dream that occurred a few months ago. In it I was standing with a dark-haired woman peer, looking at a piece of choral music by my favorite Lutheran composer of sacred music. It was a new song, which I had not seen before. As I held the score, I began to beat and phrase the music, and she started to sing an extraordinarily *lovely* melody. I was surprised to hear it, for the top voices where one would expect such a melody were sopranos and altos given homophonic phrases above a full choir accompaniment; perhaps she was singing the soprano lead for the full choir part, though I could not spot it as I conducted as though for the full ensemble. She sang on with incredible beauty, precision, and simplicity, which prompted me in turn to phrase beautifully and naturally in my conducting. I was drawn to her by a common bond of holy concern implicit in the sacred text, as well as by our shared spontaneous creation; I felt very close to her, but not romantically. She was a kind of spontaneous companion to the best that is in me.

When she finished, she turned to me gravely and asked, "Now where is *your* artistry?" meaning the composing that I had contracted with my publisher to do but had been putting off. I mumbled, and realized that I had not yet made a definite plan to start. I shrugged off her question as though with modesty, but knew that it was really a fear of failure that stopped me.

I awakened then in the night, actually weeping from the hushed and sculptured beauty of her singing, and so sure of the help of God that I began the next day on my composing, and finished a major work in a few months.

Questioned on how the dream had affected his devotional life, the dreamer responded that the phrase, "Sing unto the Lord a new song," had for years been for him the essence of active, creative faith, ever since he had seen it carved on a wooden screen in the home of a composer. It stood for man's daring, from the time of Exodus and Miriam's triumph song onward, to make new beginnings with the help of God. The "new song" in the dream had reminded him forcefully of that kind of God, One never fully contained in the forms and doings of the past, but always pushing on to new expressions of Himself, together with man, His image and partner. After the dream, the musician reported, he found himself at times approaching his periods of prayer and quiet with a greater sense of expectancy than ever before, regarding his life and affairs; he felt a nameless assurance that something surprisingly good could come about even in daunting circumstances—something as surprising as that melting melody from the unknown singer at his side.

In addition, the keen, direct question to him by the woman had provoked a sense of being known clear through, as though by the same God who numbers the hairs of the head. He had felt his defenses exposed, yet not for humiliation but reassurance, and he had felt during the dream a sense of urgency to answer the call for his own talents, while both hesitant and yet weeping for joy. The sense of being known and "believed in" by the Father, despite his defensive posturings and fears, often returned to him in his prayer life afterward, as it did in his work as a musician. He did not feel that the woman in the dream was a divine figure, but rather a kind of messenger, an emblem of promise. She felt like someone clearly other than himself, as indicated by her singing a melody he could not see in the score, and by her questioning him. At the same time, her singing a melody as an "inner voice" of the ensemble made her a bearer of assurance that the dreamer would find within his reach the inner quickenings he needed for his composing. When he prayed, he sought this same sense of "otherness" and yet "inwardness" in his relation to God.

The dream did not, he explained, make him over in some kind of psychological alchemy. In fact, as he turned it over in his mind during the night, it called forth a certain amount of anxiety, for he knew he would have to lighten his teaching load to concentrate on his composing; he would have to drop a night course he was teaching, and accept no new private pupils. The result would almost surely be financial hardship for his family. Finally, he fell asleep, and the next dream of the night, not surprisingly, dealt with his practical concern.

I was at Virginia Beach (where I had recently led the singing for a retreat, at a seaside hotel-like structure). In the dream I was in a building not unlike that one, with high, glass-walled rooms. I was talking with some peers, especially one male whom I did not recognize.

Then I went out and walked along the sandy beach (as I had recently done at the retreat). I came to a group of young people sitting in and around a low wooden enclosed area in the sand, and was about to pass them by. They were busy as though mending nets or something similar, and I heard them singing to themselves, *a cappella*. I was stopped in my tracks, for the song was an anthem called "The Rainbow Bridge of Prayer," and they were singing it in perfect balance and phrasing. It was a song I had used in church choirs years ago, mostly for its words and a climbing, lyrical tune which I had arranged to simplify it and contain its overflowing hope and romanticism. In the dream I was transfixed to hear this music and these words coming from strangers on the sand, and as I stood there quite undone, they sang a closing phrase which I had arranged as a prayer response. The quiet words were, "For so He promised us."

I felt something like a light inside me—how can I describe it? It was a totally holy thing of joyous attunement to God, in trust and gratitude.

I went up to one of the group, a young male adolescent, and asked where they had learned the music. He responded somewhat diffidently, as though determined to keep his mind on his work, that they had learned it at a hotel in Hawaii, where they had worked last summer. I did not feel rebuffed, but only grateful that they could so easily and naturally mix song and work, there on the beach.

When I awoke and wrote the dream down, I printed at the end of my notes: "A stab to the very soul: trust the promises of God and go ahead with your creative work, for unexpected resources will surely appear!"

They did, in some high-paying recital dates that followed in the next few months, requiring little extra preparation and more than making up for the income lost by lightening my teaching load in order to compose.

What had the dream done to alter the dreamer's prayer life? He reported that the very title and worship mood of the song had led him, in the months that followed, to put much more time and attention on his devotional life; sometimes, on days when he was not teaching, he took several hours to pray and meditate, before he started on his composing. The dream group of unknown singers had given him a renewed sense of "the company of God," the communion of saints, the "crowd of witnesses" who were somewhere at work in their own way, while he was at work on the often lonely task of composing. He recalled that some of his church choir singers had come from Hawaii, and found also in the dream a sense of promise that companions and fellow musicians would be available to perform his scores when he needed them.

The retreat setting in the dream, he explained, helped to remind him that his music should somehow cleanse and lift people, as well as interest and please them; with this goal he could better pray for help in his work than for career-oriented success alone. Finally, the adolescent lad reminded him of his own rebellious and sullen side, laid bare in analysis as a tendency to demand the approval and aid of adults. To see the lad undistracted came as an assurance that such qualities in him could change, so that he could hope to work for long periods without outward approval and encouragement, so long as he kept intact the bridge of prayer—the rainbow bridge.

Telling the dream, he was reminded of an earlier dream of months before, which had also emphasized his prayer life. It had come the night after he had telephoned an older man for aid in securing subsidy, so that he could compose. In the dream he went behind a switchboard where there were two telephones connected to trunk lines enabling him to call friends for aid. However, an operator silently handed him a golden phone (which in the dream he associated with excellence, not with opulence), without connecting wires, and gestured for him to use this one instead. On awakening, he made no sense of the dream, but some time afterward was struck by the notion that the golden phone was a symbol of praying for guidance, rather than begging for aid. From that time on he prayed as freely for financial concerns as for his children or for a repentant heart; he also resolved not to seek subsidy until prompted to it in prayer or in dream.

Questioned about the frequency of musical dreams, he reported that they were not common, though he could recall them as far back as his college days, when at a time of despair over his academic work and young love life he had heard a male chorus in a dream sing completely through an unknown but powerful arrangement of "A Mighty Fortress Is Our God"—leaving a lasting residue of assurance about his manhood and his faith in God.

Whatever was operative in dreams of sacred music he felt had something to do with his "higher self," and to be of the same order as that which had once led him to hear music for about twenty minutes while wide awake. That time it had been symphonic music, unknown to him, but vigorous and richly voiced. It had happened "within," for he could momentarily tune it out, but it was not subject to his control, for he could not change it. The occasion had been the period while he was waiting at the hospital and praying for his wife, as she was delivering their last child. The music had built steadily to a finish exactly at 8:15 P.M., ending with a compelling assurance that the baby had been born and all was well. He had sat there in astonishment, and wondered to himself how the shepherds at Bethlehem had heard their music. Before long the nurse had come in and told him that the arrival had been at 8:15, with the baby girl and mother doing fine. The effect of the experience on his prayer life had been to make him feel that families did not "live unto themselves," but were somehow part of larger wholes which they usually could not see or sense, in the Kingdom at once on earth and in heaven.

Asked whether such dreams were not after all merely experiences of his own unconscious, rather than of the action or Grace of God, he responded by telling another dream, where the question of what was his own and what was God's was put in abstract imagery. Prior to the dream, he had been counseling some of his singers on how to find the "direction" for each of their lives—a trajectory which would combine their vocation with their achieving the fullest individual personhood. He had taken the idea of a "life direction" from his reading, for an adult class, of Martin Buber's *Good and Evil*, where Buber had warned against the ever-present human temptation to stay in the "swirl of possibilities," insisting that there was in fact a direction for each life which a man must try to find—a personal destiny to which God called him. The concept had seemed to the musician to be promising, yet not clear, and he had returned to it before falling asleep that night, while reading the chapter on "Love" in the anonymous little book, *A Search for God*, based on discourses of Edgar Cayce.

The dream was an "insight" or "explanation" dream, of the sort which had come to him every month or so in the last couple of years, dealing with questions that seriously concerned him. But this dream, while not emotional, had for him a transforming quality that went beyond all other dreams of its sort, as it depicted two structures and then helped him to discover what they meant.

> Just before awakening in the morning, I saw two centers of action for good in the person. They were spaced apart, as if in a drawing or demonstration, yet they were very much alive.
>
> One was firmly structured in the general shape of an arc or horseshoe, with the open end pointed toward the area of consciousness in an individual. It was intricate in its component box-like parts, quite individual, and seemed constantly to tug on a person or affect his "direction" from within. It struck me that this was somewhat like the Biblical "heart" of a man, for it was a purposive, action-oriented center of forces, building the person's outward roles and style and manner, as well as affecting his individual occupation.
>
> It was responsive to consciousness and affected by it, as well as by the person's cultural setting and station in life. I remember thinking that it was historical, his own deposit of essential personhood, laid down in a particular time and place. It could not be invented, however, for its essential design was given to the person. He could only steer it, use it, unfold it, draw upon it—or ignore or damage it. I got the impression that I was seeing what in the East is called the Karma of a given lifetime, and what Buber meant by the individual's direction or destiny from God, or what Progoff meant by the "life myth" of a person.
>
> Some distance away from this structure was the other one, seeming to "shine" on the first as the sun gives its energy to the earth. It was esentially global or round, and covered with a network of nerves or vines that were intricately interworked. I was reminded of nerves and the brain, and again of living vines with hidden roots, yet this was like nothing I had

ever seen, for the center was glowing with pure light or force.

I knew that this was the soul, incredibly good and loving, overlaid with the results of all that a person had truly chosen or undergone—his particular channels for the inward fire or force. It was *as good as the heart of God!* Indeed, it was of exactly the same order of reality.

I was speechless before the radiant goodness of this structure, trying to take in the thought that everyone's soul was this pure and this great. Unlike the "heart" structure, which was meant for good but could become hardened or distorted, this structure was only capable of good.

I remember being overcome with the discovery, *"My soul loves the other guy just as much as it does me!"* And I wondered, even in the dream, how I could ever have thought otherwise, since the soul so evidently partook of God or was God, in this respect. I could see why it was important to "love thy neighbor as thyself," for any other stance would surely eclipse some of the soul's shining force, cutting down on that pouring, blessing stream which it seemed to be constantly sending toward consciousness.

It seemed that the "heart" was intimately a part of a person, active in his subconscious, while the "soul" only overshadowed him—lending its energy and quality to the "heart" and to consciousness. I could see why the Bible verse, "In patience possess ye your souls," for it could take a long time, perhaps eons, to get the whole person in line with that glowing center of goodness. One would have to seek alignment with it. And one would have to pass on its force to others, for this was too great to keep for oneself without damage to sanity.

The question of whether God was spatially *in* us seemed inappropriate. Rather, through this good soul, He seemed to be "indwelling," or "inpouring" us. Using this fabulously complex center, a little universe in itself that backs up each person, He keeps, I thought, His witness always present. I had no sense of God's being limited to this soul in His action on the person, but felt I was beginning to see at least this much of how He works with us.

The lines of channels woven into the crown of the soul were like branches of vines, suggesting specific ways, specific talents and commitments, in which each soul had become "ingrafted" in the Vine of Christ. Evidently even the soul had to grow, like everything else in creation. It seemed very, very old, and I thought I could see why the Orient could speak of the antiquity of the soul, or why Christians would speak of being in Him who was "in the beginning," and "without whom was not anything made that was made."

I do not intend to suggest that I had any kind of revelation in this dream. I just felt I was beginning to catch onto some things. It is possible that I may have misunderstood what I saw, though it doesn't feel that way. In any case, after this dream I was more helpful to my students as they probed their own "hearts" to find a life direction. And I think I have trusted something of "my own" a bit more since this dream —trusting it to lead me to be more loving and wise and creative and patient. Further, I have found myself many a time looking for hints of the soul of another person, shining somewhere behind his eyes; people look a bit different to me now.

Asked about the effect of the dream on his prayer life, the dreamer responded that it had heightened the sense of the "transcendence" of God, rather than of His "immanence" as might be supposed. For the kind of love and goodness he had glimpsed in the soul, in his dream, so far excelled human qualities as to take the breath away in awe. He found himself praying to, or approaching in meditation, this qualitative God, rather than a Being marked chiefly by his quantity of power, or wisdom, or control over the affairs of men. At the same time, he felt that after the dream he trusted more deeply in the effective *force* of God, despite his own evil or "hardness of heart." It seemed as though he could count on real aid in turning his arc-shaped "heart" during quiet times of devotion, to bring it into alignment with his—and was it his property or God's?—soul.

The dream had not been his first to deal with the relation of quality and force in the action of the divine. Some months before, after teaching a class in which he had touched on the subject of creativity in composing and performing music, he had dreamed a similar dream two nights in a row (which he reported was not uncommon for this kind of abstract dream).

I seemed to hear and perform sacred music, which embodied prayer and yet was hard work to rehearse and to sing. The dream seemed to have this particular musical setting in order to show me some features that prayer and work had in common, when done with the inner intent that God might be glorified.

Both prayer and hard work seemed to act first of all to arouse *energy* and add something to our *being*. They seemed to mediate the primal vital force that is active in us, enabling us to tackle the antimonies and absurdities of life, and giving us the ego-strength and drive to *endure*—to care, to try, to risk. I seemed to see this as part of what India had so long celebrated in Shiva, divinity both of meditation and of natural energy or fertility. I could sense better than before Shiva's uncanny and unsettling yet helpful force.

At the same time, both prayer and hard work seemed to act to add to the *quality* of our being. They bring the *richness* of wisdom, loving, strength, intuition, beauty into our doings. They quicken the hidden opposites in our creative acts, and reconcile them. They make it possible to love the Lord with all one's strength and mind and heart and soul. I thought I saw this as part of what India had celebrated in Vishnu, divinity of blessed goodness and appeal, full of the human graces.

It seemed to me, during the dream, that I was shown this tension of aspects in creativity, found in both work and prayer, because as an artist I could overvalue the richness or qualitative aspect, missing the gift of *force to live*, which came right along with the richness, and must be cultivated in both myself and my singers. Otherwise we would too often find ourselves trapped in the predicament described by Paul, seeing more and more of the good but unable to do it. One had to pray not only to be better, but just to *be there*—as in Tillich's phrase which I remembered from a book title, "the courage to be."

Later it struck me that I had been helped to understand the meanings of both "force" and "creative" in the Cayce term for God: "The Creative Forces."

Asked whether such abstract dreams were common for him, the music teacher replied that they certainly were not. Most of his dreams centered on the themes that had turned up in his analysis: work, sex, love, manhood, authority, self-worth, public acclaim, conscience. Most had plots from daily life, or reasonable facsimiles. Most seemed in the present, except when he was in a period of distress and growth, when they would more often drop back to childhood or adolescence.

Over a period of time, he reported, he found himself represented in dreams as a cheat, a braggart, a murderer, a pervert, a show-off, a fake—and also as a hero, a helper, a guide, a lover, an inventor, an explorer, and a father. Not atypical of a given week's dreams, in his view, were two dream scenes after a day in which he had yelled at his wife for failing to pay a check, at his son for failing to pick up his toys, and at his daughter for failing to come in on time after a date. Then he had dreamed as follows:

> I drive a bus-type vehicle and do a U-turn or something minor in traffic. A policeman arrests me, glares at me, takes offense at everything I say, and announces that my car will be towed downtown at great expense to me. It seems so unfair. And hopeless.

> Then I am steering a plane, and the wheels momentarily go off the runway. For this I am grounded by the man in charge. It seems unfair, with the punishment way beyond the crime.

Such dreams, he felt, added to the confessional side of his prayer!

However, his longer dreams usually contained more than a warning. They typically included some sense of the specific outcome to be sought to correct a problem. One such dream made its point in a comical way, as a crook was turned into a "good guy" by a series of accidents combined with hard work.

> At a construction job, in an indoors hall, a man sets out to steal a treasure of some sort of metal, in a bag. I see him creep and then lie on the floor, reaching out to snare some metal pieces on the floor, as the first step in his theft. He is seen and caught, and to save himself pretends to be a worker, even giving orders to others. Soon he is busy storing things in an adjoining new and unfinished storage room.

As he gets others to help him line up mattresses, he sees the
wanted treasure covered over by layers of something. Now
the thief is partly me. He is found to be without badge, and
expects to be arrested. Comically, he is lectured and told his
unit will have "1350 points deducted" because he left his workman's badge at home! He works hard, happy not to have been
turned in, although the whole situation is ridiculous since he
is not even an employee.

Now he is about to give up, as the day draws to a close and
he has not completed his theft. So he starts to drink from a
flask and his eyes get glassy. Again he should be fired, but the
boss comes out and is told he is a good workman, so he
brushes off the offense, to give him another chance. The building on which he has been working may now be seen from
outside as part of a house, in a new and modern central area.
So the crook now has a good job, in spite of himself! I wake
up laughing, enjoying the dream.

Working on the dream, the musician found that the crook suggested to him his own tendencies to try to steal professional signifi-
cance, rather than earning it. Often in campus activities he had
sought to "play the angles" by getting himself appointed to an
influential committee, or getting his choir to sing at a function
where a wealthy donor would be present, or making sure that he
was named in a student popularity poll—when he might have been
improving, instead, his work as a musician. The dream also suggested to him, in the symbols of mattresses and drinking, a tendency to want to prove his manhood with women, rather than by
professional accomplishments. However, the sense of the dream
seemed to be that life had let him get just far enough into successive
pickles, through his sly approaches, for him to have to work hard
to rescue himself and live up to what he had undertaken. Now at
last he was getting to where he could build fairly constructive and
useful professional products, symbolized by the house in the dream,
without having to be crooked at all. If there was a theological point
to the dream, and he felt there was, he saw it as the Grace that runs
constantly alongside sin, in God's unfailing efforts to pull goodness
from a man, even in his temptations. The legacy of the dream for

his prayer was thanksgiving for such aid, and delight in what he called the "humorous mischief" of God's ways with man.

The themes of manhood and redeeming Grace, he reported, had been dealt with much more seriously in a series of dreams whose common feature was a tree falling from the sky and nearly destroying him and his family. The dreams had been spaced some six months apart, and had begun shortly after he had overreached himself to become chairman of his department, at the expense of his own artistry. It took him less than a year to find that he could not handle the intrigues of campus power struggles and keep at his conducting and composing, so that he had to resign the chairmanship. In a dream which followed not long afterward, a fir tree like a Christmas tree whirled high in the air and then plummeted to earth, nearly striking him and his children at a vacation spot where they were camping.

He identified the dream tree with a mythological symbol of manhood's potency, both as a phallic symbol, and as representing that manhood which could be cut down and offered for the ritual pleasure of others—as in the ancient Isis-Osiris cult, where such a tree had represented the sacrificial devotion, by castration, made by a young man to the divine Queen Mother. The dream helped him to see, he felt, that in offering himself to the "august feminine Alma Mater" to secure dignity by the sacrifices he would make as a departmental chairman, he was repeating a life pattern of offering himself for the approval of his mother, his principal guarantor in boyhood. Such a sacrificial course had been threatening to his own talents and inventiveness, symbolized in the scene of camping, where he had always found self-reliant and ingenious ways to meet the needs of his family.

Other dreams of the falling tree appeared, seeming to him to emphasize that he could not get "up" in the masculine world or element of air by offering himself as a devotee of the powerful feminine, whether that feminine be the university, or Mother Church, or particular women such as the chairman of a faculty promotions committee, or the donor of a potential grant for composing.

Then one summer he took a good deal of time with two of his singers, newly married and on the edge of breaking up, in a marital relationship where the young man was acting out a pattern of sacrificial devotion to his demanding wife, as he had to his mother before her. The music teacher found himself spending hours of informal counseling with the young couple, more often listening than talking, but yet ready to draw on his own hard-won insights into such patterns as theirs. To his surprise and relief, the two singers seemed to catch on, and after painful hard looks at themselves, they began to build a new and genuinely happy marriage. Then this dream followed for the teacher.

> I am at a lake where I often went in my boyhood. I am with my wife, and we look up into the sky, from where we are sitting in the backyard of an unpleasant feminine relative. We see two logs flying past, high above. Suddenly they fall, one in the lake and one pinning my raincoat to the ground, as I sit there. It could have hurt me, but it didn't. While we are marveling at this near-accident (for it had seemed the logs would pass us), a young man like the one I have been counseling comes up and asks for the larger log. I say it is floating away down the lake, but I will get it for him.

> I jump nimbly on logs and sunken rocks, and with a peavey-pole I seize the log. As we pull it onto a dock, it is a *broken cross*, with part of the cross plank missing. It is long and heavy, and the wood is dark, but we pull it out of the water.

> Then the log is somehow a *dugout canoe*, over which the young man is delighted. He can take his friends in it. Indeed, before long he installs the entire log in a motor launch, and people sit in it, with decorations all around to give the thing Polynesian color, while they sip and eat and ride. He makes money with it, and serves people graciously.

> I am happy that what seemed of small account, a peril, a discard, a danger, had become a source of joy and service for him.

For the dreamer the particular boyhood setting established the theme of temptation to identify with artificial adult values, at the expense of his own, in order to get ahead as a "good boy"; the falling of the tree meant to him the danger to his manhood in such sacrificial castration.

But in this dream he was not merely passive; he was trying to help another gain the use of the log or manhood (exactly as he had been doing in counseling the music students). The outcome was a "broken cross," which meant to him a burden beginning to be lifted by following the Christ way of service. The young man in the dream who made a canoe and even a business out of the log seemed to the dreamer to signify not only his counselee but himself, as he might draw strength out of his own weaknesses and failings, to help others with theirs. In the dream, his curse had become a vehicle of blessings for the others. The final thrust of the dream seemed to be the true sacrifice was hard work for others, not castration.

The dreamer recalled, in telling the dream, that he had gone to bed thinking about a phrase he had read in the Cayce materials, to the effect that "no condition is ever lost" if given to God. He had specifically prayed to be able to turn over his weaknesses and failures to God, who might make something of them. The dream, he felt, showed him that such a process was already at work in his life, as he helped the young couple; it was a process which he described as part of the "the mystery of redemption."

Because of his reported interest in the Cayce approach to dreams, the music teacher was asked whether he had looked for seeming ESP in his dreams, where Cayce had stressed, beginning some forty years previously, that it might be found. He answered as follows:

> I find it hard to prove to myself that a given dream is "psychic," since I can usually see in it other kinds of meaning. However, there are dreams from time to time that seem to fit this category.

> For example, there was a time last year when I had taken a leave at greatly reduced salary, in order to do some composing. At one point we were at our wit's end financially, when it occurred to us to try to borrow against the estate of my wife's mother, who had recently died. My wife dreamed of three gold dollars, and felt sure that this had reference to three thousand dollars coming from her mother's estate, which was much more than we expected. We called the bank to arrange such a loan, but were told it was impossible. Then I dreamed that my wife had left some things at the bank, and that we

must return for them. The dream made such a vivid impression on me that we actually went to the bank, and inquired of the top loan officer whether a loan could be made against the estate. We found it could, and soon had the money we needed. When the estate was finally settled, it turned out to yield almost exactly three thousand dollars as my wife's share.

Was this just good sense asserting itself in my dream? Or was it some sort of a psychic grasp of affairs, better than my consciousness knew?

I found even more strange a dream about my wife's mother which I had shortly after she died. I was in the living room of a large house, in a room sparsely furnished. There seemed to be a mantel on my left. My wife's mother was there, looking younger, and playing a stringed instrument (she had been a public school music teacher much of her life). It got heavy, so she set it down like a cello and continued playing it. The music was good, even when the bow went slack and hardly touched the strings. She seemed to be enjoying herself greatly. At one point, with my wife beside her, she deliberately pulled up her long dress far enough to run the bow over a sizable white scar tissue on her right shin. The music still played as she did so, and she laughed. It was very pleasant being with her, easy and unforced. There seemed little question in the dream that it was really she, in an after-death state.

Thinking over this last dream, the dreaming man reported, he found the part about his mother-in-law playing music on her scarred shin so absurd that he hesitated to tell the dream to his wife for several weeks. When he finally did, she was excited, asking whether he knew that she had a bad burn scar at exactly that spot. He was positive that he had no knowledge of it, and added that in the dream the mother had seemed to make a point that the scarred area was well. Reconstructing events, the dreamer and his wife determined that he had not seen the mother-in-law from the time of a severe kitchen fire until her death, and had no reason to suspect such a scar. For them the dream seemed believable as an experience of communication past the barrier of death, with evidential details, although they knew it would not convince others. The effect on their prayer life was to free a bit of the strain of living, when they remembered the dream assurance of existence as a long, long adventure. And they were reminded by the dream to pray for those they loved, after death as before it.

However, the sense of meaningful dream "answers" to prayer, according to the Quaker conductor, had over the years grown out of dreams of daily problems, rather than out of seemingly "psychic" dreams. There had been the time when he had a falling out with a colleague, who seemed to him unreasonable. A dream showed him an auto accident where the vehicles represented the two of them, and he suddenly saw how his own erratic course had confused and irritated the other man, causing a near-accident in the commencement program which the other man was putting on. The dream awakened him in the night, where he lay looking up in the darkness and figuring out the entire relationship, until he could completely forgive his colleague—just as he had asked to do when he prayed before falling asleep. Or there was the dream that told him his wife needed some quiet time for her own creative work as a painter—which she confirmed by telling him that she had been nearer to inward distraction and exhaustion than at any time in the past ten years of their marriage. And the dream of an entire class walking out on his lecture, which he took to be a warning against further extension teaching, and later wished he had respected when traveling to teach the class proved to be an exhausting burden. Out of this kind of material it had become natural for him to expect that any problem in daily life on which he sincerely worked at a solution, and then prayed about it, would sooner or later turn up in dreams in a helpful light—though not always a flattering light. But he had learned to take the blows with the lifts in the dreams, for the lifts were sometimes memorable, as in this little note from his dream workbook.

> Wakened at five with a sense of being close to the Spirit of Christ, strong and relaxed. With this kind of attunement, I could face anything.

The entry was of the same character as another item in the dream book, near the same time.

Last night I awakened with a pretty clear sense: God can use my talents to get my cantata composed. I repeated the thought over and over, to be sure I had it. No revelation, no vision, but a quiet and steady assurance—almost offhand in character—in the middle of me where the good prayer and meditation experiences always begin. I knew it was a promise, and I had to trust it.

He did trust the dream promise and the cantata included a treatment of the words from the prophet, Joel: "And it shall come to pass afterward, that I will pour out my spirit upon all flesh; and your sons and your daughters shall prophesy, your old men shall dream dreams, your young men shall see visions; and also upon the servants and upon the handmaids in those days will I pour out my spirit."

Clues from Cayce

What is the potential contribution of dreams to prayer?

Can dreams anchor prayer? Can they give the dreamer convincing experiences of God at work in his life, making Him real even in His mystery, so that he may pray to Him rather than to his own imagination?

Can dreams advance prayer? Can they focus the dreamer's attention on specific areas where he needs to grow, and quicken his contrition, his resolve, his sense of how to begin, and finally his thanksgiving over gains?

Can dreams answer prayer? Can they incorporate specific responses to pleas for guidance, for healing, for aid, by indicating resources as practical as money and as precious as assurance of relationships beyond death?

Finding the answers to such questions requires thoughtful investigation, and even experimentation, in the whole range of processes called prayer. To some of devout persuasion it will seem tempting God to experiment with prayer. But to others of equally devout persuasion it will seem to have been Jesus' way to experiment with prayer—as he demonstrated the withering of a fig tree, as he invited a disciple to walk on the water, as he explained which kinds of

healing require fasting with prayer, and as he promised that know-
ing the truth could make his followers free.

Serious investigation and experimentation in prayer presumes
sharing findings, which others may duplicate or correct. But prayer
is difficult to discuss, insofar as the most intimate things of life are
not to be prattled about. If prayer is in any sense "falling in love
with the Real," then all the shyness of a lover trying to tell of his
caring may rightly be found in speech about prayer. As Erich
Fromm has observed, the ultimate address of God in faith tends to
be a "nameless stammer," which Judaism has hinted in its prohibition of the name of God. Insofar as prayer is speech to God, rather
than speech about God, it may well be found difficult to report to
others.

Yet the effort to investigate and to share must surely be made.
Some of the investigators of prayer will be naturalists, collecting
and arranging specimens as did William James in his study of
religious experience. Others will investigate by constructing models of the body and psyche in transpersonal divine fields, as boldly
as Freud constructed models to leave out such fields, and will sup-
port the models with painstaking case materials that may hope to
approach Freud's. Still others may concentrate on instrumenting
prayer and related phenomena, using the electroencephalograph so
fruitfully employed in dream study, or using projective devices and
comparative states induced by drugs. Some will attempt to isolate
prayer variables and sets of variables, studying them in loosely-
fashioned projects (such as the project from which the musician's
dream material in this chapter was drawn), or even developing
controlled experiments similar to those used on such other altered
states of consciousness as hypnosis, sleep, and sensory deprivation.

But all such careful inquiry is likely to develop only in the presence of a "lore" of prayer among thoughtful, critical people. When
there were enough informed and balanced people able to report on
their own experiences, psychoanalysis became more than a Vien-
nese cult, hypnotism more than entertainment, and Black Studies
more than a slogan. So, too, the progress of the study of prayer is
likely to require disciplined, patient inquiry by many who are not
content to seek inspiration for their personal devotional life alone.
From their joint venture may come fresh approaches to prayer,

modeled not on the spell nor on the plea at the foot of an autocrat's throne, but upon such diverse images as the response to a song, the wakening from sleep, the touch of hand upon hand, the tuning of instruments to play, the flowing of ultrasonic waves, and the force of pure light in laser beams.

There are many directions in which clues may be sought in the investigation of prayer. There are the ecstatic rituals of primitives, the experiments of Olds in localizing a brain center in rats which appears to give more pleasure than sex, the ascetic practices of monks, the manuals of yoga, the best experiences of those taking LSD to enter what Cohen has aptly called "unsanity" rather than insanity, the experiences of Boisen and others mentally ill as they regain their balance, the times of highest creativity reported by artists or by scientists such as Pauli.

But surely one of the most unlikely direction in which to look would seem to be the discourses of an unconscious man, and a man with a grade school education at that.

Yet as William James both argued and showed, one effective way to approach a too-familiar phenomenon is to show it in its exaggerated forms, where all its tendencies are magnified. James adopted the method for his lectures on the varieties of religious experience, where he included striking cases from the life of prayer. It is also the method of this book, which takes up one exaggerated, nearly impossible case in the history of prayer: the work of Edgar Cayce on dreams.

Edgar Cayce, who died at his home in Virginia Beach, Virginia, in 1945 at the age of sixty-seven, was not peculiar in his personal devotional life. Over the course of forty years of his adult life, as these years are reflected in his diaries and his thousands of extant letters, as well as in several hundred recorded dreams, he seems to have prayed about much the same concerns that other people pray about. He prayed about money, about integrity, about sickness, about sex, about his children, about the two world wars of his lifetime, about his faith, about his wife, about his vocation. He had his inward struggles, and he tried to deal with them in daily Bible reading, prayer, and meditation.

But he also had an outward, public prayer life.

For while he had the vocation of a photographer—and he was a good one—until his mid-forties, he took up after that age a vocation so strange in twentieth-century America that it bordered on the impossible, and fully qualified him as one of the extreme cases that William James recommended investigating. He took up a vocation of full-time counseling in and through a prayer-induced trance state.

At the age of twelve, while reading the Bible through for the thirteenth time (beginning a lifelong practice of reading it through once for each year of his age), he had prayed to be able to serve as had others in the Biblical narrative, and he had received what he felt was an answer and a promise. Beginning the next day, and continuing until the end of his life, he found that he could enter a special state of consciousness by praying, where he could secure information helpful to others from what in time seemed almost an inexhaustible supply. He called his source simply "the information," and used it for most of his life to accomplish medical diagnosis and prescription.

When, in his forties and afterward, he tried to gain prayer guidance on subjects as diverse as the economies of nations, the chemistry of the blood, the location of buried oil fields, the psychological predispositions of a newborn baby, the meanings of specific dreams, the political groupings in ancient cultures, and trends in real estate and earthquakes, he continued to describe his prayer-induced counseling as "readings" and was told by experts that he was in "self-induced hypnotic trance" where he functioned as a "psychic diagnostician" or "traveling clairvoyant." He took the labels in stride, and went right on praying and sharing what came from him in prayer—whether in the heightened consciousness that sometimes marked his teaching of Sunday School classes, or in the unconsciousness that marked his twice-daily trance readings for persons usually not present.

To the end of his life, he saw his unusual counseling experiences as a chapter in his prayer life, where he thought he was enabled— in the words of Paul which he sometimes used—to be "absent from the body and present with God."

He did not claim divine authorization for what came from him in his various prayer states, awake and asleep. Instead, he early became convinced that he was doing nothing new in human history. He thought he was using lawful processes available in some measure to any man who sincerely prayed—and lived and worked as he prayed. He often told others, including the present writer, who studied him at first hand for eight months, shortly before his death, that "I don't do anything you can't do." During the last two decades of his life Cayce made a special effort to coach others to draw from their prayer life as much as he drew from his, and achieved striking results with the creative output of two businessmen in particular, and later with the members of a small study group and a prayer group—as well as in lesser measure with members of his adult church school class in the Presbyterian Church, and with members of a Tuesday night Bible class in his home.

Whatever else he may have been, Edgar Cayce was a praying man who taught others to pray. He was also a man who kept transcripts of everything he said in prayer-induced trances for more than twenty years, perhaps as a photographer keeps negatives of his photographs. His materials, consisting of some thirteen thousand "readings" with associated correspondence, medical reports, engineering reports, archaeological reports, and case records of trainees, constitute what is probably the largest single body of prayer materials in Western history.

Whether the Cayce records also constitute valuable prayer materials is of course open to investigation. In the last analysis, their value is quite independent of their source, except as the source— a man in an unconscious yet highly lucid state initiated in prayer —may have usefully exemplified particular prayer processes. The ideas in the Cayce readings may prove sound, even if Cayce's personal prayer life be judged unbalanced or immature—which it certainly did not seem to the present writer. Or the ideas in the Cayce readings may prove erratic or worthless, even if Cayce's own prayer life proves to biographers to have been rich and profound. As William James insisted, the value of a set of ideas or procedures must be judged "by their fruits," not "by their roots." The discrimination is important, to guard against the tendency to project upon Cayce's obvious sincerity and piety a stature for his counseling which it may not deserve, when weighed item by item in careful scholarship and research.

But the Cayce records do make a fresh starting point in the study of prayer. They are so unusual that they are like stained tissue, which may be examined with ease under a microscope. They are so extensive that they touch upon every aspect of the life of prayer —and in fact upon many major processes of growth, change, and decay in the body, the mind, and society. They are set in individual counseling discourses, which gives them the weight of concrete case materials, though it also gives them the weakness of unsystematic development of idea. They employ Cayce's own vocabulary and value system (with exceptions that are congruent with these), so that the records may fruitfully be studied against the background of the man's life and mind and times. They do not have the character of vague generalities from a supposed master on another plane, although they suffer all too often from the grammar of the waking Cayce, trying to describe what he saw and felt in the altered state of consciousness to which prayer brought him.

And the Cayce materials have the merit of working out in casestudy detail, through several hundreds of his trance expositions, the way in which specific dreams respond to and contribute to the life of prayer. They provide a useful if unusual starting point from which to examine how dreams may anchor prayer, may advance prayer, and may answer prayer.

CHAPTER 2

Working
with Dreams

The modern study of dreams began with the publication of Freud's monumental work, *Interpretation of Dreams*, at the turn of the century. The book appeared at the same time as that other landmark study of subjective materials, James' *Varieties of Religious Experience*, but Freud's volume developed a framework of dream theory which left little place for the divine More that occupied James.

Dream study in the first half of the century was associated with the consulting room, although Freud and those who followed him in exploring the language of symbols soon turned to interpreting myth, rite, art, and literature, with the same procedures used on dreams of the ill. Many of the studies undertaken by Freud's successors showed great sensitivity in handling such religious themes as rebirth, sacrifice, death, and love, while Freud himself caught with painful clarity the sense of being divided against himself which is the lot of any maturely reflective man. But the relation of dreams to prayer and meditation received little attention from medical psychologists.

Then at mid-century, starting in the 1950's, a new approach to dreams was developed. As is often the case in science, the new research was initiated by discoveries in instrumentation—chiefly the use of electrodes to indicate when eye muscles were twitching in sleep (the time that soon proved to be the period of active dreaming), and the use of electroencephalograph equipment to demarcate four levels in sleep, as these were reflected by brain waves. With new instruments, scientists had devices for catching fresh dreams in the laboratory; soon they began painstaking studies of the length of dreams, their placement during the night and in the scheme of brain wave levels, the effects of depriving sleepers of dreams, the recall of dreams, how dreams reflect experiences of the previous day, whether ESP impulses can be received in dreams, whether people can be trained to perform tasks without awakening, when sleepwalking occurs, how drugs affect dreams, and scores of related questions. Dream study became a respectable part of "hard" or academic psychology, where before it had been limited to the "soft" or speculative psychology of the consulting room.

But the emphasis in laboratory study has tended to fall on the form of dreams rather than on their meaningful content. Not because scientists are uninterested in the meanings of dreams, but because few interpretive frameworks are available for approaching the rich language of symbols. Any handling of symbols makes scientists as uneasy as when they are interpreting love or faith or art or play—in all of which symbols are critically involved. As might be expected, the correlation of dreams with prayer and meditation (processes which are not yet well instrumented) has received little laboratory attention. However, the laboratory study of dreams has turned the study of dreams into one important new direction which may stimulate correlations with prayer and meditation: the study of dreaming by subjects who are not neurotic. The typical subjects of dream laboratory tests and research are harassed students, rather than the mentally ill, and there are indications that the dreams of these students may include material closer to the content of prayer and meditation states than has been the dream material recorded in consulting rooms.

Halfway between Freud's work at the turn of the century, and the mid-century innovation of laboratory dream study, there developed the major part of Edgar Cayce's work on dreams. It was work which produced absolutely no response in the scientific community, not because Cayce's dream interpretations were poor or unbalanced (later research, such as the present author's *Edgar Cayce on Dreams,* has given them serious attention), nor because of wide divergence from Freud (like Freud, the Cayce source insisted that dreams were the royal road to self-discovery for modern man), but because the idea of an uneducated man interpreting dreams in a prayer-induced trance state seemed absurd.

Post-Cayce study of dreams in the laboratory has uncovered the remarkable ability of some subjects to interpret their own dreams with considerable sophistication while under hypnosis. Had Cayce done his work several decades later, he might well have been studied for his hypnotic interpretations of his own dreams, if not the dreams of others.

But there were things that Cayce did with dreams in the years 1924 to 1932, and in lesser degree up to his death in 1945, which might have made even seasoned laboratory dream researchers avoid him.

What could be done or said about a man who could not only interpret the dreams of others read to him while he was unconscious, but could recall for the dreamer entire dreams he had forgotten on any given night, locate the time of night the dream occurred, and correct errors in recall? What could be said of a man who frequently predicted correctly what his subjects would dream next, even on occasion naming the exact night or time of night?

What could be done or said about a man who regularly tagged some dreams as detailed representations of future events, from the birth of a baby to football scores, from auto accidents to the death of friends, not excluding stock market developments and business deals not yet conceived? While it was useful to his dreamers that Cayce could do these things (even adding further helpful details of future events to nudge the dreamer along), his performance would have bewildered many a research worker.

And how could sense be made of Cayce's ability in trance to instantly correlate the dream with all sorts of events and structures in the dreamer's life, from his earliest childhood to his most secret affairs, and from his kidney condition to the state of his bookkeeping or investments? The entranced Cayce operated as though every aspect of the dreamer's biography, as well as a good deal of his future and his unknown present surroundings, were open to Cayce for swift correlation with dream material.

Finally, how would research proceed with the Cayce claim that the basic function of each night's dreaming was to compare the trends of the dreamer's daily life with the commitments of his "soul"—a structure that has had no status in either the consulting room or the dream laboratory, however long its history in theology? To work with the Cayce dream materials requires considering a universe where God and Christ are as real as nightmares from overeating, and prayer and meditation are as natural as sex.

Over the course of about twenty years, beginning in the mid-twenties, Cayce gave some seven hundred of his prayer-induced trance readings for nearly seventy people who wanted their dreams interpreted; he dealt with approximately sixteen hundred and fifty complete dreams. Ninety per cent of these dreams were submitted by four persons, one of whom was himself, so that the resulting body of Cayce dream materials has exceptional case-study depth, as well as suggestive breadth of distribution among dreamers.

The correlation of dream material with prayer and meditation runs all the way through the Cayce dream documents, but exists in two levels. Prior to 1932 the emphasis was on developing dream depth and skill, with prayer and meditation approached somewhat instrumentally to these ends. After that period the emphasis was reversed, with primary attention given to development in the spiritual life, especially by members of a study group and a healing-prayer group; for them the material on prayer and meditation received first attention, with dream study made instrumental to growth in prayer.

What was the approach of Edgar Cayce, in his altered state of consciousness, to the use of dreams in normal daily life?

Recall of Dreams

While it was still widely doubted in scientific circles, Cayce in trance was insisting that every normal person who was not ill dreamed extensively every night; he proved it to dreamers by recalling their dreams for them. Recent laboratory research has borne him out, suggesting that most people dream about an hour and a half every night, in what is usually four well-separated dream periods, with the longest period just before waking (and the one sacrificed by people who cut short their sleep from the one-third of each day which Cayce and laboratory researchers agree seems necessary).

It was the contention of Cayce in his hypnotic state that every normal person could and should learn to recall his dreams, so that he might study them for clues to better functioning in his daily life. The reason for such recall and study was not that everyone had a constant battle against neurosis, although the Cayce "information" handled many dreams not too differently from the way psychiatrists would. The reason was rather that the Cayce source saw many, many dreams as adaptive in nature, problem-solving for daily life, rather than as engaged solely in psychiatric rescuing or transforming of the psyche. In this view, the "subconscious" was often busy processing the concerns of waking life: health, business, friendships, travel, a philosophy of life, purchases, hobbies, churchgoing, card games—whatever genuinely engaged waking consciousness. Invention and problem-solving in dreams were not the prerogative of inventors and artists alone; everyone did it in some measure, every night, except when he was ill or sorely troubled—when dreams had to be occupied with rescue and growth of the dreamer more than with his world of affairs and activities.

This perspective made it reasonable for dreamers to work at recalling and using dreams, rather than waiting for a breakdown to drive them into it. They could expect from their dreams practical interpretation of each day's events: how they really felt about a business associate, how they honestly viewed their diet, what they had often overlooked about a child. They could also expect brand new material in their dreams: an indication of an unknown illness of a relative, the exact figures at which a stock would sell, the address of an apartment for rent, the face of a businessman yet to be met, the amount to be paid for a vacation house, the details of a theft by an office boy, a coming epidemic or tidal wave or war. Further, they could expect in dreams something not yet identified in research on dreams before or after Cayce: systematic nighttime tutoring on matters in which they were interested. Blackboards, schools, teachers, books, churches and temples, groves—all of these would often be found signaling dream material whose purpose was to instruct the dreamer in some process important to him: often the nature of his own selfhood, but sometimes the nature of the American banking system, or of life after death, or of cellular operation in cancer—and sometimes the nature of prayer and meditation, and of the Lord whom these addressed. If all of this material were available in dreams, as well as the self-regulating and self-healing and self-growing material which made up that part of dreams more familiar to psychiatry, then learning to recall dreams made sense.

The first step in recall of dreams, for the Cayce source, was the same as the first step in the interpreting of dreams, and the first step in learning to pray or to play the piano: a decision on one's purpose. The approach of the Cayce readings was similar to that underscored by modern research on LSD: in matters of creative and transformative material from the unconscious, "set" would be found crucial. Purpose would determine whether much was recalled or little; if one sought to use his dreams to succeed in business without growing as a person, he was not likely to get far. If one sought his own growth without looking into dreams for ways better to serve and aid others, he would not get far, either. In the view of the Cayce trance source, it was always the "ideal" chosen by the person which affected what the deep mind would give him, asleep or awake.

But there were also practical steps to take in recall of dreams. Beginning dream students ought to write down their dreams every morning (and some found it better to do this when wakened by a dream at night). Rehearsing dreams as soon as they were recalled, running over them in the mind, even at night, would move them more permanently into the memory. One Cayce reading pointed to an aspect of recall which sleep laboratories have recently confirmed: recall would come easier before the body was moved around. Finally, one could tell himself as he drifted off to sleep that he was going to remember his dreams, so that he could use them helpfully in his life; or better, he might pray for this outcome, as God saw best for him.

There were hints in the Cayce materials that recall need not stop with remembering the scenes and characters and moods of dreams. One could learn, with patience, to recall the actual reference of all these symbols at the time they were being dreamed—or at least their general intent. Then, on awakening, one might begin inter-pretation with some symbols falling open like ripe fruit, as rapidly as one handled them. Or one might recall the concern behind most of the dreams of a particular night—the same concern which mod-ern laboratory research suggests may be at work between active dream periods, setting up each dream to come. For the Cayce "information," the guiding concern in a given night appeared to be determined not only by the current events and trends of the life, to which the dreams were responses, but by the dynamic center of the personality, the "soul," which presented the sleeping psyche with the original dream stimulus through the "superconscious" (that part of the unconscious which had direct access to the soul and to the divine), after which the stimulus was elaborated by the "sub-conscious" into dreams. The impression was given by the Cayce source that many or all dreams were in principle "suggested" to the dreamer by his own soul, as a hypnotist can by suggestion produce dream themes in a given subject.

Recall, then, was not mechanical retention of odd material from the night, but potentially a growing conscious participation in the total action of the dream process, while it was going on, or before or after it. "In patience possess ye your souls" could be found literally true in dream recall, if the work with dreams were matched by an active life of service, guided and cleansed with prayer and meditation.

Interpretation of Dreams

Richness of recall which included recall of the reference and intention of dream segments would constitute impromptu interpre-tation. But one could verify interpretations even while asleep, ac-cording to the Cayce source; a dreamer could at times send himself back to sleep to dream the interpretation of a dream that had wakened him. Or he could listen for a voice—and this was less common—which would be his own higher self or soul addressing him, and succinctly commenting on dream scenes and events. Even when these interpretative procedures were not working for a dreamer, however, the Cayce source encouraged the practice of running over dreams in the mind, as one might pull a magnet through a tangle of metal pieces, to organize them on lines of magnetic force. Uninterpreted dreams, too, could be useful to recall and ponder. They might do their own uninterpreted work of alerting the dreamer to a peril, or to an opportunity, or to a process which he needed to understand. Even as primitives may perform rituals that appear to nourish them psychologically and spiritually, though they give no rational account for their doings, so the Cayce source appeared to view dreamers as gaining from going over dreams, to let them be heard in the consciousness of day as they had been heard in the night.

However, there were some dreams which did not need interpreting, according to the Cayce readings. One group of such dreams which the Cayce "information" identified is still inaccessible to modern laboratory or clinical research; these were dreams described as never fully reaching consciousness, and yet doing their work in the economy of the psyche (perhaps hypnosis, or drugs, will someday bring such dreams to light). The remainder of dreams not needing interpreting were merely symptomatic, not intelligible in themselves. Such dreams, in the view of the Cayce materials, originated in abnormal body chemistry (all dreams, in the Cayce view, appeared to employ body chemistry, under the stimulus of endocrine secretions—such as those secretions recently identified in laboratory research as producing male penile erections nightly with dreams which may have no sexual content). The uninterpretable dreams would be found to lack dramatic structure, what the Cayce readings called "heads, tails, and points"—and what Aristotle called "beginning, middle, and end"; they could result from foods eaten, from fever and illness, from anesthesia, and from injuries that affected endocrine secretion and other aspects of circulation.

The great majority of dreams, however, could be interpreted—and best interpreted—by the dreamer himself, not by either an analyst or a psychic such as Cayce (however helpful both kinds of counselors for starting a dreamer on his dream study).

As the entranced Cayce interpreted dreams, he began with their function. They could be found to operate in one of two ways—or in a combination of these two ways. Some dreams were primarily concerned with advancing the dreamer's practical effectiveness in the concerns of his daily life; these problem-solving dreams were the province of the "subconscious" which held the dreamer's habits, body functions, style of life, and immediate practical problems. Other dreams were clearly concerned with changing the dreamer, with improving his commitments, enlarging his self-image, enhancing his understanding of life, or even relating him better to God. Such dreams were primarily the province of the "superconscious," though mediated to the subconscious for the actual dream production on the screen of consciousness. Still other dreams contained elements of both kinds of dreaming: problem-solving and transformative. Such mixed contents might appear in successive portions of one dream, or more often in layers of meaning of the same dream symbols (as Freud so well demonstrated). In any case, dreams were "answers" to the life of the dreamer. While they might contribute no more than a delineation of a problem in the dreamer's activity or makeup, which was in itself a potential help to him, in general they also held the seeds of guidance for his next steps, and these seeds should be sought out. But such seeds could only be found by laying the dreams alongside the real life and personhood of the dreamer. Interpreting dreams was interpreting dreamers, finding what function was performed for the dreamer by specific dreams, or by nightsful of dreams, or by a dream series.

The beginning of dream interpretation, then, was self-inventory, to discover what was on the dreamer's mind, whether in the forefront of his worries or in the dim recesses of his guilts and fears and hopes. Only with such inventory, often repeated and modified, could dreams be found to make sense. For such self-study, the purpose or "set" or ideal of the person made a difference; if he were hiding from himself, his inventory would be inaccurate, and he would either get no dreams or few dreams—or he would get repetitive dreams, hammering away at something which needed facing.

One step toward determining the function of given dreams—how far problem-solving and how far transformative of the dreamer —would be paralleling the dreams of a given night, most of which would develop similar themes. One could also trace similar plots and characters in dreams occurring over weeks, months, or years. Using sets of dreams in this way, one could proceed as does a cryptographer: using gains of interpretation made in one dream to illuminate others similar to it. Like Carl Jung, the Cayce source advised the study of dreams in series, not in individual dreams alone.

But locating the general reference of dreams was hardly enough, although much might follow at once, in sensing of whether the dream were a warning or an encouragement, a lesson to study or a guide to action and decision. (Quick hints to such dream meaning may be found, as modern dream research has suggested, by asking about climax scenes, tag lines, and memorable objects or events, as well as by asking how the dream might well have been different, and what such a difference would suggest.) Sooner or later, one would have to grapple, too, with the reference of specific symbols.

In the Cayce view, there were three kinds of symbols in dreams. There was literal material, referring to just what the dreamer saw in the dream (such contents would be what psychologists call "signs"). Frequently, literal material appeared in dreams of practical affairs, in dreams of the future (the Cayce source noted that nothing important ever happened to an individual which was not first previewed in a dream), and in dreams of health concerns; usually this literal material was mixed in with nonliteral material— although very rarely a dreamer might see a scene of the present or past or future exactly as in reality (and the Cayce readings referred to these scenes as "visions").

There was metaphoric material, which the Cayce source called "emblematic." Usually dream contents operated much as do daily speech, where a portion of something stood for a larger whole (feet for one's footing, ship for the vessel of one's life journey, automobile for automotive stocks, gun for threat), or where an item from one area of experience stood for an item of another (storm for storming about, gun for male sex organ, jeweled bracelets for holding a treasured child in one's arms, lost in the woods for confusion of thoughts). In the view of the Cayce source, most dream material of most people was emblematic; such material compressed many kinds of meaning into specific images, and also served to motivate the dreamer for action, better than would verbal dream essays. Much emblematic material dealt with outer affairs and concerns of the dreamer, but by far the largest portion of it dealt with his own subjective or psychological concerns—his talents, defenses, habits, ideals, fears, stereotypes, emotions; for this reason, it was often useful to begin interpreting a dream on the assumption that most of the people and events in it represented trends and structures in the dreamer himself.

Finally, there was mythico-poetic material in dreams, which the Cayce source called "visionary" (and which modern psychology might call "true symbols" or "ikons"). This material did not have simple reference, but appeared in dreams because of its capacity to awaken and arouse the dreamer to meanings he had not yet grasped; it was important exactly because it could not be translated in interpretation, but must be lived with (as the cross, the sun, the fish, an angel, an unknown beautiful woman as a guide, a spinning sphere). While many of the images and actions used in dreams at this level might also function as emblematic (the cross for a church, the sun for tan, fish for fishing), study of the context and mood of the dream would indicate the extent to which it was visionary. The function of visionary material was primarily to transform and orient the dreamer; this material came primarily from his own soul and the action of his superconscious responding to the divine. However, material which was visionary could also have with it emblematic and even literal layers, to be found only by patient study and response to the feeling and thrust of the dream, in relation to other dreams, and to the dreamer's life.

Several of Cayce's major dream subjects sent him, along with their dreams, some of their material from waking life: fantasies, slips of the tongue, moods, compulsions, promptings, irritations, phrases that ran in the head, and quickenings from their prayer life. The Cayce "information," as did Freud, traced this waking material to the same sources as dream material (though Cayce differed from Freud on some of the sources), and encouraged dreamers to use waking signals and symptoms, and states where the unconscious dominated, as further clues to the meaning of similar material in dreams. More than once the entranced Cayce recalled to a dreamer that he had been musing deeply on a certain subject, or reminded of a problem by a passing sight, on the day before his dream; by such comparisons one could learn, he said, how dreams worked.

The Cayce "information" also suggested specific types of dreams for which dreamers might watch. There were dreams with a cast of characters of friends and associates, where the dream would show the attitude of each one to some common concern or problem, or to the dreamer. There were review dreams, going back over considerable periods of the dreamer's life to show him how he had handled sex or power or vocation or an Oedipus tie—and to suggest next steps. There were roadmap dreams, laying out the major directions for a dreamer's growth in the next period of his life. There were signal dreams, heralding the coming of something important in his dreams, often the beginning of a cycle of dreams on a given theme. There were tutorial dreams, training him in analysis and application of some particular area of his life. There were promise dreams, assuring him of his relation with his Maker, and of his ultimate destiny and worth as a person.

How could a dreamer learn whether his interpretations of his dreams were correct? There was no simple rule. But obviously the overall progress of the dreamer's life and affairs was relevant, for dreams were meant to aid him, to grow him, to relate him to others. At the same time, internal criteria needed to be used as well, to validate the interpretation of dreams. Successive dreams of similar content should be studied to discover whether they showed progress—whether an animal or an emotion was being tamed, a partnership represented as more harmonious, the dreamer's manhood stronger. But there was also the appeal to a special aid in validation, alongside of all other criteria—not in place of them. That was appeal to "the still small voice" within. One could pray for the meaning of particular dream passages, after working hard on them (not instead of working on them); then one could put down the dream content and go about his way, secure in the assurance that the next time he set out to study his dreams intensively, something helpful would occur to him—or that he would dream the dream contents in a new and more helpful way. The Cayce source insisted that meditation, regularly practiced in a specific way, would act especially to open an ever-clearer channel to dream interpretation, as to guidance of every kind in the life; dreamers were challenged to try this out experimentally.

One who took his prayer and meditation seriously, working at them as faithfully as he worked at his dreams, would find—if he were also acting in a constructive and productive way in his daily work and loving—that his dreams improved markedly in clarity and usefulness. As the Cayce source showed the major dreamers with whom Cayce worked, their dreams grew more terse, they grew more accurate on factual matters, they reached further and further into the ultimates of faith.

Prayer and meditation were, however, no magical key to working with dreams. Equally important was to use something of what was learned through dreams, to try out the interpretations in decisions and activity, guided by quiet reflection and study. Nothing would stimulate and improve dreams like using them responsibly —though using them as omens and oracles for every little action would shut them down, to preserve the balance of the person. Useful was the making of one's own heraldry from dreams (as Carl Jung had long encouraged his patients), including life seals of repeated positive emblems, and the choice of jewelry and clothing and colors in the light of dreams. Important, too, was the development of balance in every aspect of one's life; even diet, and certainly exercise, would be found to have specific reflections in both dream content and form, while recreation and study and play would be found to have their own necessary balance, intimately mirrored in dream quality. Yet because dreams were ultimately under the control of the soul, they needed especially to be worked with alongside prayer and meditation.

In such a process, said Cayce from his prayer-induced state, it would be found not only that prayer and meditation aided the recall, interpretation, use, and improvement of dreams. It would also be found that dreams could aid prayer and meditation. They could anchor prayer, by disclosing to the dreamer in his own convincing imagery the work and Presence of the real God, with Whom he had to do. They could advance prayer, by pointing the dreamer to the next concern, and the next, on which he needed to seek Help greater than his own. And they could and would answer prayer with concrete guidance and healing energy, responding both to the prayerful life of the dreamer, and to his earnest intercession for those he loved—or knew he should love more.

CHAPTER 3

Working with
Prayer and Meditation

Modern research on prayer and meditation has until recently been limited to libraries. Ever since the translation of the Hindu Upanishads by the Frenchman, Anquetil du Perron, in the early nineteenth century, there has been a continuing Western interest in reading of Oriental modes of prayer and meditation, now and then given impetus by such Easternizing groups as Theosophy, Anthroposophy, and Vedanta. That impassioned and articulate lecturer, Vivekananda, at the Chicago Congress of Religions just before the turn of the century, left an impact on many in both the United States and Europe, while a half century later such Western scholars as Suzuki and Watts opened up afresh for Western interest the devotional practices of Zen Buddhism.

At the same time, scholars have continued their exploration of the West's heritage from monastic devotional life, as well as from periods of quickening that spread to laymen, in Catholic Quietism, in early European pietism and in Methodism, as well as in the

American Great Awakening. The discovery of the Dead Sea Scrolls, and the tracing of early eighteenth-century practices of East-European Hasidism, have both contributed to the recovery of the heritage of Jewish devotional life. Meantime, interest in faith healing has periodically prompted new or old prayer practices in church life, and the remarkable success of Alcholics Anonymous has called attention to the use of prayer in small growth groups—such groups as have often been the center of what has been called the modern "Renewal" movement in both Catholic and Protestant circles. The use of prayer in nonviolent civil rights demonstrations has had its place in quickening interest in ancient devotional practices, while Hindu nonviolent philosophy has brought with it to Western campuses both Indian music and Indian meditation.

Still, neither scholarship nor experimental lay efforts have constituted research of the sort familiar in dream study by both clinicians and workers in dream laboratories. The exception in prayer study may prove to be modern inquiry into psychical phenomena, which engaged the interest of William James as it has many others since his time because of its possible illumination of prayer and related states. Using both field methods popularly called "psychical research" and laboratory methods called "parapsychology," this investigation has sought to discover not only how man's mind may reach the future, the distant, the past, the dead, but—as Rhine and other researchers have made clear—the divine itself. Little formal research has been reported on parapsychological aspects of prayer and meditation as such, but such research questions have never been completely out of sight.

Only since Hofmann discovered LSD 25 in 1948 has modern science begun to pay systematic attention to "altered states of consciousness," other than hypnosis and mental illness, in ways that make possible serious study of prayer and meditation. The reports of mystical experiences with psychedelic drugs, when such experiences are sought and prepared for, have become common enough among responsible and religiously mature people to allow the assumption that drug states may parallel mystical states enough to allow the study of the one to stand in for the study of the other. As in dream research, the breakthrough has been instrumentation —in this case with drugs the instruments for inducing possible prayerlike states, or for heightening tendencies to such states. It seems likely that the near future will bring further instrumentation of the prayer-states achieved, through the use of electroencephalograms, and through the development of projective devices which allow the sorting of prayer-states. But already permanent gains for research have been made, in discoveries that good and bad experiences for the same users of psychedelic drugs are brought about less by the drugs than by "set" and "setting"—the purpose and expectancy and understanding in the drug experience, combined with the field of loved or respected people participating in an attractive and symbolically suggestive environ. This discovery has led to fresh exploration of set and setting in prayer and meditation, with renewed interest in the possibility that small chemical stimuli (such as sacramental bread and wine taken after fasting), or natural body chemicals (produced in states of concentration in optimum set and setting), may be involved in religious states of altered consciousness.

Edgar Cayce's readings appear to have taken account of prayer and meditation from an early date, although the subject only received systematic treatment in the last dozen years of his life. Throughout the first two decades of his use of a prayer-induced state, he gave medical readings almost exclusively; yet these same "physical readings" may have included some form of psychosomatic counsel in as many as 75 per cent of their number. Usually such reference was made to the attitude of the patient and those about him, but there were also recommendations of hypnosis, self-analysis, self-discipline, recreation, and other procedures which the Cayce "information" insisted affected the body as significantly as did medication or surgery. Prayer and meditation were mentioned and enjoined often enough to lead some seekers to request a special type of reading from Cayce, called "mental and spiritual" readings, whose content was an analysis of the basic spiritual health of the individual, as well as recommendations for growth in prayer, in Bible study, and in full stretching of the self for service of others.

From 1924 to 1932 the few individuals who took Edgar Cayce's work most seriously, and helped most assiduously in developing for him a complete Cayce Hospital and Atlantic University at Virginia Beach, Virginia, were mostly Jewish. They responded to the ideas in the Cayce materials, including the emphasis on prayer, but they had to work at their growth largely as individuals, for the Cayce emphasis on Christ made it impossible for them to develop study groups within the framework of temple or synagogue life with which they were familiar. As a consequence, they sought readings chiefly on topics of dreams and psychic ability, as well as on life after death, where concerns of prayer and meditation were incidental—such as the Cayce source insistence that the living should pray for the dead rather than simply seek counsel from the dead through psychic communications.

The 1929 Depression brought its strains to this group of backers, mostly wealthy businessmen and their families and associates, and mostly in New York. Unable to work together through these strains, they lost the hospital and the university, and most gave up their contacts with Cayce. At this point Cayce's training work through his readings shifted to a small group of interested people, largely church people of modest means, in his surroundings in Tidewater, Virginia. For the next dozen years until after his death, Cayce did his best counseling work for these people and their families and friends—perhaps a total of twoscore close associates. For all of them, guidance on prayer and meditation, especially as it might be developed in small study and growth groups, became central. They did not all work equally hard at it, and some were more interested in the Cayce source treatment of their supposed past lives, in the entire theory of reincarnation which emerged in the Cayce materials. However, the central thrust of Cayce's work in this period was clearly on prayer and meditation, with associated Bible study and the undertaking of disciplined lives of growth and service. One small group received scores of readings from which they compiled two little devotional manuals of their own thoughts and experiences stimulated by the readings; they called these *A Search for God*, Books I and II. Another small group, an outgrowth of the first, conducted healing prayer for the sick, and sought several dozen readings on the processes of healing through prayer and meditation, over a period of years.

What were the ideas on prayer and meditation which emerged from the Cayce trances?

The Twin Processes of Service and Attunement

Again and again the Cayce "information" insisted that there were two great commandments for man: service, and attunement.

Service meant service of one's fellows, in all the real doings of everyday life; it did not mean merely religious service. The key New Testament phrase offered in the Cayce materials was the saying of Jesus, "Inasmuch as ye have done it unto one of the least of these, ye have done it unto me," and the Cayce source insisted that this phrase was literal; the soul of every man was sprung from the same Godhead as the soul of Christ. The key Old Testament phrase used was the question of Cain, "Am I my brother's keeper?", and the key to every man's prayer life was suggested as his own version of a phrase which he could repeat or think or act out many times daily: "Lord, let me be a channel of blessings to others, today, now." Using what purported to be retrocognitive clairvoyance, the Cayce source described what it saw of the life and work of Jesus, as well as of his associates and predecessors and followers; of Jesus himself the Cayce "information" said that his most common prayer was "Others, Lord, others." The Cayce trance materials presented the figure of Jesus in terms not far from the classic phrase of Dietrich Bonhoeffer, who called him "A man for others."

True service required much more than a string of good deeds, in the Cayce trance view. It required the best of man's brains, talents, love, opportunities. Each soul was a portion of "the Creative Forces, or God," though only a portion. But as such it had untold possibilities for good, both in this life and beyond, in other lives or stations. What was required was disciplined application in the use of one's talents and station; service meant that the musician made better music, the carpenter better benches, the legislator better laws, the housewife a better home, the psychic better readings. Most men were not serving at top capacity because they were not growing at top capacity, nor motivated at their top capacity for love. Service also meant relating to others so as to bring out the best in them, rather than exalt oneself—a perspective in which the Cayce source set the example by its treatment of Cayce himself: he was not to be made the center of a sect or cult, and people were not to be high-pressured to join his modest service organization, the Association for Research and Enlightenment (though its development was the subject of many helpful readings for its leaders). Service was more than promotion. It was, in fact, the ultimate destiny of man, who had one day to become no less than a co-creator with God, by choosing service in every realm of his experience for eons of time, until he could "have that estate with Him which was in the beginning, and be conscious of same." Through service one became a conscious companion with God, far more than a pawn of the divine. Through service one took the precious gift of free will and made it a wellspring of beauty and truth, love and holiness, from "the Creative Forces" always available to him according to the measure that he actively used them for others.

But because service involved the welfare of others, even the welfare of Nature and the angels, blind activism was not enough, and love could be as possessive or destructive as freeing. So the other great commandment must be observed, for a man's giving to his brother to be truly wise, truly helpful, truly creative. This was the commandment of attunement. The key New Testament phrase used for this process by the Cayce source was the saying of Jesus to his disciples, "I go to prepare a place for you, that where I am ye may be also," and the Cayce emphasis was on a place "in consciousness" rather than in geography or astronomy or occult planes. The promise was that every man could attain, through time and patience which might require millenniums (but should not), "that mind which was in Christ Jesus," by drawing on his own innate "Christ consciousness" and by direct attunement to the Other One, "the Christ" who stood ready to help him on the human journey which He had also made in full. The key Old Testament phrase for attunement was the Hebrew prayer called the Shema, built around the phrase, "The Lord thy God is One," and the emphasis of the Cayce materials was that man could, by attunement, make his own human will and creative energy come into oneness with the unspeakably creative Force of the divine, who alone knew how service should best be conducted—how all things might "work together for good" in each situation. And the prayer motif so often enjoined by the Cayce materials to underscore attunement were the words from the mystical experience of Isaiah, full of the sense of the very Presence of God, when the stunned and cleansed prophet answered, "Here am I; send me." No less than sending by the divine was the fulfillment of attunement promised to every man, a sending which could one day be as consciously known as was Isaiah's, but only if its thrust were service.

Attunement through Prayer and Meditation

Attunement was the image used by the Cayce readings to describe generic prayer—the heart of all individual and corporate worship, in whatever form. Such attunement was always attunement to God, though the thought for the moment might be chiefly on one's brother, or upon a work of art or a garden. It included attunement to one's own soul, and to the fullness of Creative Forces which surrounded the soul for its use as airwaves surround a radio or television receiver. Such attunement could awaken memories of the best one had ever known, of the highest ideals he had ever chosen, and of the examples on which he could model his life—ultimately Christ himself. But the various mechanisms involved in attunement were not as important as the effort itself, made in quiet, made in martyrdom, made in beauty, made in despair. Whatever the form, and forms were useful and important, the intent and spirit of attunement was foremost in determining its effectiveness. One had to live as he prayed, or his spirit was insincere, and would not quicken his attunement; in psychological terms, not making things right with one's brother would create unconscious blocks to impede the flow of energies, in prayer or in meditation.

In the view of the Cayce source, there were definite processes in attunement. Within the individual, attunement followed the same physiological and psychological avenues used in all creative work, play, study, or loving; whenever the individual was absorbed, rapt, fully alive in a creative task or relationship, he employed the same processes that he called forth in worship. Accordingly, creative service kept the way open for attunement, just as attunement kept the way open for service.

Concretely, the Cayce source described a chain of reactions within the endocrine gland system of the body, as these interacted with both cerebrospinal and autonomic nervous systems, to bring about all creative absorption, including attunement. (These claims have only recently met some confirmation, in research on the relation of sympathetic and parasympathetic systems to endocrine function, both in creative activity and in the fighting of disease and the maintenance of health and growth.) The terms used to describe creative absorption by the Cayce source were drawn from Hindu kundalini yoga, and the imagery of "wheels" or centers of force at seven points in the body appeared to bear a direct relation to the visionary material of Ezekiel, as well as to late-Judaic apocalyptic material such as that in the Book of the Revelation. Over a period of twenty years, the Cayce material on the physiology and psychology of creativity, including all attunement of prayer and meditation, became an impressive collection of data, worked out in detail in individual cases and correlated with disease, injury, age level, dream activity, and many other variables.

Within the broad generic process of attunement were two primary subprocesses, those of prayer and meditation, each of which —according to the Cayce source—had its own function but needed the other. How the two might best relate could be seen in the Cayce counsel of one procedure available for an individual seeking to begin on a serious prayer life. Such a person was often encouraged to take thirty days to get his prayer and meditation started, by getting up each night at 2:00 A.M., when he could not possibly be disturbed by others or by duties requiring attention. In this time he was to take the first half hour for prayer, lifting his heart and mind to the Father through every means that he understood and cherished: especially thanksgiving, but also confession, adoration, aspiration, dedication, petition, intercession, and other inward and outward movements of his being Godward, which had been hallowed by centuries of praying men. He might read the Bible, or devotional sayings, if he did not let this reading substitute for actual prayer—and the Cayce source often recommended Exodus 19:5, Deuteronomy 30, such Psalms as 91 and 103, and John 14-17, as well as many other passages specifically commended to individuals. The seeker could pray aloud, which would be found helpful to most, or silently; he could pray on his knees or sitting or standing. It was not methods which counted, but the use of approaches which truly stimulated the deep devotion of the individual toward God—and each one must find his own way. Some might use incense or candles or lights or music, and some might cleanse themselves and put on special garments. All would be well advised to use the same place for this opening training, returning to it each night, for the body and the mind required habits to aid in deep absorption.

But after this half hour of "concerted effort to attune body and mind to God," then an equal period should be given to meditation. In this emphasis the Cayce materials departed from usual Western practice, but they were insistent. If prayer were turning Godward, meditation was receiving. If prayer were asking a question, meditation was opening the way for an answer. If prayer were stilling, then meditation was conception of new life within the being. If prayer were filling the consciousness with awareness of the Being and Will of God, then meditation was emptying consciousness so that the Very God might enter in, making Himself present "in, with and under" the body and mind of the believer, precisely as Christians had long signified the presence of Christ in the sacramental elements taken into their bodies by eating and drinking. In the view of the Cayce source a definite action took place in meditation which was essential to the life of prayer, not just interesting or optional. Energies moved, however unperceived at first. Nerve connections were refashioned, glands were cleansed, ideas and values strengthened, until in time the meditating person would find himself operating from entirely new bases within his being (as William James had said, it would be as though a polyhedron had tipped over onto a new side).

If meditation were so valuable, why not skip the prayer? The Cayce source insisted that meditation was an act of communion with God, not possible unless the consciousness were filled with and focused on God. While some might enter into spontaneous meditation at times of joy or suffering in their lives, experiencing its full action, most people needed to know with Whom they were meditating, in what spirit or purpose—and prayer determined this. It would be possible to "raise the energy" of meditation by other means such as intense concentration, or even with drugs, but he who did so without placing himself wholly at the disposal of God, at every level of his being—as in heartfelt prayer—did so to his own undoing; for the same energies meant to be quickened to bless and grow and refresh him could also disorient him (and in the view of the Cayce materials, much of mental illness involved the same kundalini activity as did creativity and attunement). In meditation, the essential action taking place, in the view of the Cayce readings, could be caught in the words of Paul, speaking for the divine, "My Spirit beareth witness with thy spirit." Choosing to find and to know this "bearing with" in meditation, the individual would find the witness more quickly and surely when next he needed it for acts of service. Prayer would aid him in attuning to the Most High, rather than allowing the rush of impulses from the unconscious, or even of telepathy from the living or the dead, when the silence of meditation was entered.

The Cayce source often enjoined quiet reflection for individuals, suggesting that each must learn to "step aside and watch self go by"; it even recommended the use of columns of ideals on a piece of paper, where one might sort his spiritual, mental, and physical ideals and correlate them. Self-analysis through dreams, and through honest and loving sharing of appraisals in families and in group work, was urged, just as the Cayce source appeared to value its own counseling aid and at times recommended professional aid for individuals needing psychiatric assistance. But such reflection was not "deep meditation." Such reflection should be conducted at some other time, if one were to carry out the approach recommended for the 2:00 A.M. hour. For the meditation recommended to everyone by the Cayce source was not the usual thinking at all, and not even praying; it was nondiscursive, not thought, not analysis, not weighing or rehearsing of ideas. Instead, in meditation one sought to practice attending to the divine, stilling, waiting, clinging. The action beyond this attending was not up to the individual at all, but up to God, who would do what He would do—and would not fail, though it might be long before the individual knew what God undertook with him in the stillness of meditation.

As an aid to holding the mind still, to not thinking in meditation, the Cayce readings offered over the years several hundred little prayers, called "affirmations," such as the two following:

Create in me a pure heart, O God. Open thou my heart to the faith Thou hast implanted in all that seek Thy face. Help Thou mine unbelief in my God, in my neighbor, in myself.

How excellent is Thy name in the earth, O Lord! Would I have fellowship with Thee, I must show brotherly love to my fellow man. Though I approach Thee in humbleness, and have aught against my brother, my prayer, my meditation, does not rise to Thee. Help Thou my efforts in my approach to Thee.

Individuals were encouraged to put the thoughts of the affirmations into their own words, and to use these thoughts or prayers at other times than at meditation, as well as to think them out carefully, phrase by phrase. Biblical language was characteristic of these little prayers, as though the Cayce source wished the praying person to confront the whole force of the company of the faithful, the people of God, when he set out to humble himself before the divine in meditation. More than "positive thought" was intended, for the affirmations characteristically included some indication of the individual's powerlessness or sin without God. And more than self-development seemed intended, for the affirmations always carried some reference to service of others. These little formulations were terse, because they were to be used as a quiet focus for the thinking mind, as a place to hang thought, so that the intellect could be still in meditation. The affirmations themselves were not the business of meditation, for that business was no less than direct communion with God, by allowing Him to "enter into" one's holy of holies, within his inmost consciousness. To the Cayce "information," the entering-in of God through meditation was not merely poetic, but real; some actual change always took place when meditation was properly and faithfully undertaken, in a setting of earnest prayer preparation.

There were hints of the activity in meditation that an individual might notice before long in his meditation periods: tinglings, loss of awareness of limbs and senses, currents along the spine, warmth and fullness in various areas of the body. When meditation reached its full cycle in the individual, it would often culminate in a gentle floating on the breath, while the whole field of consciousness seemed filled with light, and the self absorbed in deep stillness—with a joy that would seem to many to transcend all other joys, in its certitude of the reality and love and presence of God. For meditating itself was not the goal; the receiving of God into one's heart, one's flesh, was the goal. Meditation was only a means, and the signs in the body and the mind only useful for encouragement or warning along the way.

The fruit of meditation might in some cases be felt at once, as the energies that had moved in the body went on about their cycle to cleanse and balance the very organs of the body. One could find old resentments gone, fears melted away, sadness released. In the view of the Cayce source, this action in meditation was not mere emotion, nor suggestion, for concrete changes were taking place in the very nerves and glands of the body, as well as in the mind. If one went on to act and to serve in the spirit of this freeing, begun in meditation, he would indeed be different, for this action—aroused in meditation and released in constructive and loving action—was nothing less than divine Grace. Such Grace was not blind or capricious, but within man's reach, though not always apparent in his consciousness. It was the means by which forgiveness was activated, the means of "new life in Christ," the means of permanent change for old habits and "the old Adam," taking place in the very physiology of the person.

At the crown of meditation, which would not for most people come suddenly, but would in time come for everyone who persisted, would be found a filling-up, a quickening, a sense of "being met"; in the view of the Cayce trance source, this was the action meant by the Biblical phrase of "being filled with the Spirit." That it was often accompanied by sensations at the top of the head, or in the forehead, only indicated the wisdom of ancient traditions of tongues of fire on the head. What one was here encountering in full form in meditation was no less that the entering of the Christ Spirit, a separate Force from that of one's own soul, but a Force or a Person always ready to answer, to aid, to enter in, when the way and the life—the whole quality of the life—were prepared for Him.

In the Cayce view, meditation which followed prayerful attunement, and was engaged in regularly and at sufficient length (at least fifteen minutes to a half hour daily; longer for some who sought to train themselves for service through prayer), would always bring its changes in an invisible field which made up the "real body" of a person—that same body which would at death be the "risen body" for him, and which was acted upon in prayer healing (as it had been acted upon in the resurrection of Jesus). Still using the metaphor of attunement, the Cayce source spoke of "vibrations" which would be raised in the individual during his meditations—spiritual vibrations yet real energy, found also in creative and loving activity. When this vibratory energy was "lifted up" in prayer and meditation, it needed to be given out, so that the closing act of the period of meditation might well be intercession for someone else, the giving of a blessing. If one sought to keep the energy for himself, he ought not to expect it to return, for the force that moved in meditation was from God, and giving was its character.

Could meditation yield guidance? Sometimes a flash of a certainty, or a new birth of love, could follow at once upon meditation. But to seek these during the meditation time, or too closely afterward, would be to distort the action. When God was invited, one did not tell Him how to behave. The effort to turn meditation into a time for guidance, or self-improvement, would only block it. Too often the anxious unconscious would flood the mind with images, whether of the order of dream material or of psychic material; any images at all would be a distraction away from the desired still emptiness before the Throne. Better, in the view of the Cayce readings, was to go forth from meditation secure in the knowledge that guidance would come the next day, and the next day, as it was needed—a little more clear and wise and refreshing each day. The proper follow-through on meditation, then, was to act, to serve—but yet to pause before entering each difficult new task, and quietly to renew the contact made earlier in the lighted silence, asking whatever was needful for that task or relationship. Guidance would come, and only fear or cruel doubt or misuse of opportunities would shut it off—not because God went away, but because the psyche darkened its own door by turning against the best it knew.

After thirty nights spent in trying this cycle of prayer and meditation, what then in attunement and service?

The Cayce materials suggested much more. Working with a study group was encouraged for everyone—a group which would share the real life of its members, exploring existential themes and setting out tasks to be tried experimentally between meetings. The members in such a group ought to pray for each other by name daily, as often as possible at agreed-upon times, as they should also pray for others bound with them in the bundle of life. Such group activity was the heart of what men sought in church and synagogue, not replacing these ancient institutions, but giving them their life-blood. Further, each group would be found to build up from its shared activity and common ideal—if the ideal were a worthy one —a force that was greater than the force of any one member, and a force which could be joined with the Christ force for intercession. There would be found, said the Cayce trance source, both prayer of "defense" where others were afforded protection, and prayer of "offense" where energies were set in motion to change the very cells of a sick body, or to tug a confused mind toward the Light.

Each person's journey in prayer and meditation would be his own, as he found the ideas and the procedures and the promises that brought him alive before his Maker. But each one's journey was properly made in company with those of like mind, as well as in behalf of those who had no use for him or for his meditating. For it did no good to pray for, nor to love, only those who prayed and loved back. God loved each, and his servants must do likewise— daily, often.

New times would be found for prayer and meditation—especially those hours of the morning when the body and mind were fresh. New hints of what was important in corporate worship or spontaneous play or beautiful art or struggling with crisis would emerge as one carried with him the touchstone of his times of prayer and meditation. More and more he would see that he was not "mastering" prayer and meditation, but was beginning to "walk with the Master." For the gift of prayer and meditation was not mysterious powers, but "that Light which was the light of men"; it was not religious wonders, but the One.

If prayer and meditation took their beginning and ending in God, where would He be found?

The Cayce trance readings encouraged study, encouraged the use of religious traditions, encouraged the formulation of religious laws and principles—so strongly as to seem to make every man a theologian. Yet these studies were to be understood as offering only stimuli and guideposts, in this view. For "all that ye may know of God is within"; it was a claim which did not belittle learning, but rather insisted that in matters of God, man had to "get understanding"—and understanding came from quickening beyond the rational mind as—and only as—that quickening was matched by study, by practical application, and by risking in daily life. One could know of God, with certitude, only so much as he had lived out with others—though he might surmise much else. Yet if he were bent upon ever-fuller comradeship with the divine, which had called his soul into being to be no less than God's companion and co-worker, then he might receive gift after gift of the divine Self-disclosure, Self-sharing, for his own active life of service.

One avenue of the divine Self-gift was dreams. The Lord of Hosts, sought and celebrated in prayer and meditation, as He was sought and celebrated in worship and teaching, had not forgotten man in the night, when man's mind was still. There He would make Himself known, as of old. And man could waken to pray aright.

PART TWO

How Dreams
Can Anchor Prayer

CHAPTER 4

The Time
Is Fulfilled:
Dreams of Destiny

The Gospel of Mark records a terse saying of Jesus which may well have been the heart of his preaching. The saying appears at the start of his ministry, after Jesus has been baptized, spent forty days in the wilderness struggling with temptation, and learned of John's imprisonment. Coming into Galilee to speak with his fellow countrymen, Jesus said, "The time is fulfilled, and the kingdom of God is at hand; repent, and believe the good news."

The saying easily becomes trite for modern ears. It is heard as a slogan, as ideological, as churchly. But it is stamped with four dimensions of faith, dimensions so rich as to afford the basis not only for Jesus' ministry, but for all authentic prayer. These dimensions may be used to measure the contributions of dreams to the life of prayer.

The first of these dimensions has to do with God's action in time: "The time is fulfilled." Modern ears hear this claim as mere Biblical rhetoric, telling how Christianity was predicted for centuries by

Old Testament prophets. Or, with more imagination, moderns may hear the claim in the Hegelian terms which inform Marxian historical dialectics: thesis has met anthithesis, and synthesis has arrived. But all such attempts to read the phrase as a timetable may miss the thrust of Jesus' remark. For he speaks of time as fulfilled, as pregnant with itself and about to deliver. He speaks of timing come to an end, of predicting that is over, of computing that falters before the scope of the event: God brings forth His reign among men.

The announcement signals a shift of focus, a shift away from clever timing and predicting of events to the meaning in the events. It is a shift difficult for modern man to make, accustomed as he is to commentators and inside dope, where second-guessing events is more important than understanding them. But it is a shift which must be made, if the hearer is to catch the intent of Jesus' teaching the "coming" in fulfilled time of the Kingdom. He tells his hearers to pray, "Thy Kingdom come." After his death they teach, "All things work together for good, to them that love his coming," and they pray that simple and marvelously urgent prayer, "Lord, come quickly!"

The affirmation that the time is fulfilled points to one dimension of God's work with men: the eschatological dimension. Things are working toward an end, toward God's end. Our times are in His hands. Events have a meaning. Destiny is real. Human existence is not a trap. *Something can happen!*

On the one hand, the eschatological motif carries a sense of the unpredictable wildness, the radical freedom and goodness of God, which cannot be measured by anything yet known, but only glimpsed from the Endpoint of human doings. That something can happen means anything can happen—and probably will. God is more good than man knows how to ask or expect, and He shows His grace in swift and sudden surprises. The Surpriser is Lord of the Eschaton, not of nostalgic Eden.

On the other hand, the eschatological motif carries a sense of God's order, of His design and control within events from the moment of creation. This God is not mocked; He gets Himself glory even from human evil. That something can happen means Someone can happen, that His Will is at work, as in heaven so in earth. Man journeys through time with One whose secret ordering laughs at man's timing, for to Him a thousand years are but a day, and creation is done in a week with a day to rest and muse.

The characteristic prayer response to the eschtalogical may well be longing for *obedience*, to come into alignment with the unspeakably good purpose. "Use me!" "Not my will, but thine, be done!" The prayer is to keep the Law, to so live that the Name which needs no hallowing is yet hallowed. The prayer desire is not to disappear in servility, but rather to stand fast in such bonds of holy intent as to be under orders, while crying as did Martin Luther King, Jr., "Free at last, free at last! Thank God Almighty, free at last!" The dare is to be able with Augustine to "love God and do as you like," in a love which delights at obedience to the Coming One.

The Cayce materials constantly stress the note of the "coming" of God. A typical bit of encouragement in a reading runs, "As you take the first step, He prepares the way. And He will not withhold any good thing from those who love His coming." Another reading affirms, "It is never too late to mend thy ways. Life is eternal, and ye are what we are today because of what ye have been. Yet ye are a co-creator with your Maker, in order that ye may be present one day with all those who rejoice in His Coming!" The coming described is not simply a historical occasion, though the concept of the Second Coming of Christ is not belittled, but it is first of all the coming of the divine into consciousness—in oneself and one's brother.

> The law will be fulfilled. Will ye do it, or leave it to someone else? These should be choices. Will ye seek to know the law? For the Lord hath not willed that any should perish, but hath prepared ways of escape. He who seeks will find. He who knocks, to him it will be opened. These are irrefutable, these are unchangeable laws.5244-1*

In the Cayce materials, the response to the coming of God, to His reign over events as over hearts, is ever obedience—the same obedience seen in Christ.

Thus He who came into the earth as an example, as a way,

*Numbers appearing after case material designate documents on file in the archives of the Association for Research and Enlightenment (ARE), Virginia Beach, Va.

is an ideal—is *the* ideal. They that climb up some other way become robbers of that peace and harmony which may be theirs by being at one with what He manifested in the earth.

As soon as man contemplates his free will, he thinks of it as a means of doing the opposite of God's will, though he finds that only by doing God's will does he find happiness. Yet the notion of serving God sits ill with him, for he sees it as a sacrifice of his will. Only in disillusion and suffering, in time, in space, and with patience, does he come to the wisdom that his real will is the will of God, and in its practice is happiness and heaven. 2537-L-1

If dreams can function to anchor prayer, then one dimension of dream action would be a quickening of the dreamer's sense of the eschatological—of God's working purposefully with all creation towards His final ends.

When such dreams were clear, they would call forth the dreamer's understanding of a cosmic Work, proceeding in a time beyond timing. When such dreams were vivid, they would call forth the dreamer's prayerful cry for obedience, that he might hasten the Coming.

The Cayce source interpreted the function of certain dreams in precisely these terms.

One dreamer saw himself at his grandmother's grave, where there were "living stones"—a New Testament image.

Went to the cemetery with my mother, and there saw the gravestones in earth, but stones and earth seemed to be moving. I wondered at that. Then came to Grandmother's grave. We looked at it from behind iron fence or bars. Where has she gone? What has become of her?, I asked, gazing through the bars at the grave. The voice answered, "She has become part of the elemental forces that make up the whole harmonious Universe." Again I asked the same question, being puzzled by the reply. Patiently and more distinctly came the same reply. ... Not yet fully comprehending, I put the same question in a different way, and again in clearer, more distinct fashion came the same response. 900-89

Commenting on this dream, the entranced Cayce described it as a vision, brought about by the dreamer's studies on life after death, to give him a "clear, definite fact," as shown by the voice that repeated the idea three times—as in Biblical visions. The sense of the dream was that "nothing dies," with each portion of the person going to its appointed realm at death, "just as the earth is a portion of the Universe, just as an individual is a portion of the great human family, just as the spirit a portion of the great I Am." It was a dream in which the dreamer could glimpse how even at death, all things work together in God's time and way. The dreamer himself sensed the motif of cosmic order, for he asked in the same reading about an earlier dream.

> What relation have these words, "harmonious Universe," to another dream months ago of a whole orchestra all playing different instruments—all dressed in white, yet all in tune and in perfect harmony?

The Cayce source assured him that this dream, too, had shown him that the universe has but one Force, expressing Itself in earth, in family relations, in the human spirit which survives death. "All one force. One spirit force, one harmonious force, each varying in the degree of their ability to manifest the whole." The orchestra combining sounds into rich harmony had been an image of the free order of the divine at work with man.

The image of the orchestra stayed in the mind of the dreamer as an emblem of the harmonious workings of the divine, for some weeks later he dreamed of it again.

> Seemed to be in a school building and on my way to ... [a colleague's business] office. Stopped outside of the door to a classroom in which an orchestra was practicing. I heard the music as I listened at the door and wanted to go in, but concluded I had better be getting along. "They are only practicing anyway," I said. 900-117

The unconscious Cayce reminded him that the classroom setting, as in other dreams, emphasized "truths" or lessons, in this case an answer to the dreamer's tendency to separate his work from his study of religious and philosophic questions, which he valued more highly. He needed, in his daily "practice" like the orchestra's, to

"Gain, then, the full conception, through such lessons, of the one-ness of the forces as are being manifested to the entity ..." by a God who was Lord of work as of study and beauty. It was a similar lesson to one more dramatically given him in another dream, a few months later.

> I beheld a great advertisement in electric lights shining out on Broadway. It said, "The substance of matter and of mind is one and the same thing." 900-302

The Cayce source spoke encouragingly to the dreamer, one who was tempted to value the realm of mind over matter, saying, "This truth, and the understanding of same, should be emblazoned on the minds and hearts of people, even as such lights, such [advertising] conditions give to those on this [Broadway] thoroughfare the knowledge, the understanding, of what is to take place within, see?" The reading continued: "All matter is as one matter. All time as one time. . . ." Man would find that every phenomenon in his experience only expressed its original impulse from God, "its por-tion of that first Creative Energy that impels its own propagation, in time, in space, in the material form and manner." The dreamer was being helped to see all things in God, so that both his life and his prayer might be properly grounded in devotion to a Lord of Nature who was also Lord of History.

In the view of the Cayce trance source, dreams functioned not only to evoke a sense of the divine at work in creation, but to quicken an appropriate response in the dreamer. A man whose father, now dead, had become for him a symbol of his highest aspirations, asked about "my father as I always see him in my dreams, paralyzed and sick in bed." The response from Cayce in his altered state was that this dream image, actually a memory of the last illness of the father, came repeatedly to underline an "en-tanglement" of the dreamer, where his "physical actions" with women were "in opposition to the lessons taught" by the father. The lesson intended for the dreamer was that he "must keep mind, soul, and body pure, clean, unspotted from the world—presenting the temple[the body of the entity] holy and acceptable unto Him, *which is but a reasonable service.*" The intention was not asceticism but service, "Not in ... becoming a recluse, but giving of self, of body, of mind, to the developing of self and of others." For such service discipline was needed, not only over the appetites, but over pride, as was shown in the next dream of two nights later, with a "tall figure draped in white, around which were a vast sea of souls; his rebuke when I asked questions about God."

The intent of this dream, said the hypnotized Cayce, was to show the correctness of "the strong imperative" toward "seeking of the knowledge of the Father, of God ... when used in the proper channel." But there was a warning also, regarding the spirit of the dreamer's religious studies. That same knowledge of God

> may become destructive to self when ... one would become bigoted, or self-endowed with a super-consciousness of lording over others. Knowing [God] then, in humbleness of soul, of mind, of body, do we gain the manifold knowledge of the spiritual world. For God is spirit, and we must worship in spirit and in truth. 900-13

The dreamer was strongly encouraged to study his dreams for knowledge of God, "that such knowledge as gained through dream, manifestation, vision, may be given to a dying world" so that "people who would again approach the Living Way, the Living Water, may be ... established in the Holy Way that leads to [life] everlasting." By learning from his dreams, and by his service and his prayer, the dreamer could draw from his "inmost feelings, the inmost life" that which would be the very opposite of superiority over others, making his "countenance, the physical exhibition of body, of mind, such that all who behold may know *this one* has approached the throne, and brought away the shining light—ever the light by night and the cloud by day." Nothing less was the full promise of the life of prayer, where the dreamer might be found "presenting self in that manner that all [dreams and similar] manifestations will become [for others] the way that will lend strength—shrouding doubt, fear, disappointments, distrust in the depths—[becoming] such a way that only the true, the holy light will shine unto the end, guiding many to the way that leads to life everlasting." It was a strong promise of the aid of dreams in reaching a devout, obedient life with God in the service of others.

Much of God's cosmic and final work with man might be shown in dreams and visions, according to the Cayce source. One dreamer reported:

I beheld the universe and souls leaving the earth to become part of other phases or elements of creation, and also beheld souls entering to become part of the material element of creation, i.e., the earth world. . . . I saw the earth world as a round steel mass above me, and saw souls becoming part of that mass. . . . The Voice said, "Now at last you are doing my work." 900-279

The interpretation from the Cayce "information" was that this had been a vision, meant to reveal how souls who sought to point the way to "the sons of man" were so to speak "rising" to become wholly one "with the Universal or the Creative Energy," and then "returning to the earth experience for the application of those conditions gained, or for that [purpose] of manifesting again and again those truths or lessons as are gained." But the dreamer had also seen, in the souls entering the steel mass, "those that become, through the nonapplication of truths, [trapped in] the purely material conditions in the earth, and are of the earth-earthy." He would have to choose his own lifework, as the voice suggested, to exemplify the bondage with God which was freedom on the steely earth.

Through dreams it was possible to view the cosmic drama unfolding. But such dreaming, according to the Cayce source, meant little if it were not accompanied by insight into loving service of others. One dreamer of Jewish extraction, who wondered how to present the teachings of Christ to his fellow Jews, reported a vivid dream which began with the death of his brother, from whom he was inseparable, though he was not on good terms with his brother's wife.

My brother died of a stroke of apoplexy, having burst a blood vessel. I became heartbroken over it, so terribly affected that even my brother's wife put her arm about me to sympathize. 900-189

The prayer-attuned Cayce indicated that by this intense dream experience the dreamer was being helped to gain "the full knowledge of what the death of the Savior, Redeemer, Jesus meant to the world," for He had been the Brother whose death was a force to draw together the separated—as the dreamer and his brother's wife. In the personal blow of loss of the most loved one, the dreamer could begin to sense the Crucified Loved One whose simple teachings of the Fatherhood of God could draw all men together. For the true final hope was what the dreamer reported in the close of the dream, when the tragedy of the brother's death changed the scene to a theological confrontation.

> Before me appeared many sects of the Jewish faith, the Orthodox impanelled in one partition, the Reform in another, etc. All the tribes of Israel divided into rich, poor, strict, liberal, etc., rising in tiers before me, and I at their foot viewing them —teaching them, free of the barriers that hedged them in. I strove to bring them together, but many turned their faces the other way. Their inherited prejudices were too great. Then God, or the divine of God within me, directed me, and I heard the direction in that which sounded like a voice, saying, "Teach them the *Father idea* advanced by Christ."

The focus on the simple Fatherhood of God, said the Cayce source, would indeed be the helpful approach for the dreamer's task, for it always would be necessary to emphasize the oneness of God to reach the Jewish people. But it should be understood that the Fatherness meant the unison of force and purpose of "all who would come to the unison of purpose with That Force called ... and termed God—which is, as we see, merely [a term] in the mind of man [standing for] that as is set to represent that All Powerful Force ... manifested through the physical conditions seen in the physical world." As the dreamer worked with this understanding, he would come to understand why Jesus had taught that salvation must be offered, "First to the Jew," and "then to all that will harken." For, to the Cayce source, it was part of the divine plan, part of the secret workings of the Lord of the Universe, that in each generation as fresh teachings and work were presented to the glory of God, these must first be offered to the Jews. Even Cayce would not be allowed to offer to a wider group whatever might be found good in his readings, until he had worked intensively with Jewish leadership—as he did from 1924 to 1932. The Lord of the Eschaton kept his covenants, from generation to generation, as the dreamer was being shown.

Corporate Destiny in Dreams

Within the guiding action of that Providence who knew how to
fulfill time, in the view of the Cayce readings, would be found the
destiny of human groupings, human institutions. For it was as Jesus
had said, that no man held a position of power or of servitude except
by the will of the Father who allowed it to be so.

> As has been given, no man, no individual, finds himself in this
> position or that in the material world, save by the Grace of the
> Father-God. And these are the words of the Master, not from
> here. 3474-L-1

But such destiny would not be blind fate. It would be purpose
within freedom.

> . . . For, as has been said, and is given here: The higher forces,
> or God Himself, know not what a man may do with his own
> will from day to day! 311-MS-9

> . . . The entity chooses. What is your God? The Creative
> Forces, or Self? A good time, fame, fortune? You must know.
> You must answer. God does not even answer for you. He
> gives you free will to use as you choose. For He does not want
> [anything] other than that you *choose* to be equal with Him.
> If He had to knock you in the head to do it, or if you had to
> become an automaton and be pushed about, could you be
> equal with the Creative Forces? Answer within yourself. 2981-
> L-2

One of the functions of dreams would be to disclose what was
properly destined, which the dreamer might then choose. For there
was not only individual destiny, there was destiny together, pattern
within which men might work out their free choices. There was
pattern in families, as this wealthy dreamer saw.

> Then my mother, wife, and I took an automobile ride, and I
> observed all the things that money could buy, and also ob-
> served the glory of the True Life. I saw trains and boats, and
> also the entrance to what seemed a monastery. I said to my
> mother: "What is the use of making money and these things
> the object of life, when they aren't even real?"

Speaking from his prayer-induced state, Cayce reminded the dreamer of a New Testament saying: "Though a man gain the *whole world* and lose his own soul. ..." It was true that money and belongings had their place, but that place was in a larger service. "Not that each in its sphere is to be belittled, but that each is made to serve its intent and purpose, to magnify [God's ways with man] even as He would magnify."

The dream proved prophetic in disclosing a central family issue. In a few years the dreamer was a millionaire, but his family was split; he lost both wife and son.

Cayce himself had a strange dream of the destiny in his own marriage. It came four years before his death, which was followed closely by the death of his wife (as an earlier dream had predicted).

> Dreamed I was looking over a lot of records, and I saw what would have happened if Gertrude and I hadn't gotten married. She would have died in 1906 of T.B.; I would have died in 1914 from stomach trouble.

It was the same theme as the dream of more than seven years ago, where the promise in their marriage had been affirmed.

> Drove car with Gertrude through narrow passage, over muddy place where many other cars had stuck, and came to clear water and nice road.

The reading which he sought to interpret this dream told him that the plot and setting of the dream had come from anxiety regarding a contemplated trip, but that the intent of the dream was to underscore what could be done in their marriage and work together. They knew full well "those troublesome conditions that arise, as seen by the emblems of the gorge, the rocks, and the narrow road, and also those journey's along life's way where much muck, mire, and the like are emblematical of things [within] that make for the hindrances, the falling away in the experiences and the lives of others." But if the car of their lives together were prayerfully "guided aright, kept straight in the narrow way," even when they themselves doubted that the journey was worthwhile, as in a portion of the dream that Cayce had seen but not reported (an example of the reading correcting a dream report), they would come out

together as the clear water had indicated, in "the clearness of understanding, purity of purpose," where the road would be the acceptable quality of their lives before the Giver of Life.

There was a destiny for every man, and aid for him as well. This
was what one dreamer saw, who had been pondering what would
become of those who had died after wasted lives. His dream included what the Cayce source described as an authentic vision of
Christ, the sort that could ever afterward help to anchor prayer. It
began by showing him a quarrel in his own family. Then this
followed:

> I passed through a dark cellar and up into a lighted room,
> where I beheld Mrs. B. (just deceased and for whom or whose
> soul I had prayed that night), seated with many others. (I felt
> her presence on a previous afternoon, when a family quarrel
> had followed.) She said to me, "I will not have discord in my
> house. I will not have lack of harmony and trouble there."
> Then I saw many in the Borderland whose mental application
> and physical endeavors in the physical [body] had held back
> their potential development. I asked: "Who will bring them
> back?" Then a change. I felt and saw as I had once before,
> when my mind rose into the Holy of Holies, even unto the
> throne. I beheld Him as a young man this time. He was naked
> to the waist. . . . I asked: "Who is that young man?" "That,"
> I was told, "is Christ." "Who will bring them back?", I asked
> again. Christ spoke to me directly, saying but two words. He
> said in reply: "I will." 900-351

The Cayce "information" linked the plot of a quarrel with earlier
dream material, where the dreamer had seen the necessity for
straightening out his own life in respect to self-indulgence; the
dreamer had become divided against himself as a family divided in
its own house. The dark cellar and the lighted room had contrasted
what might be found in life beyond death, depending on what the
dreamer or any man had prepared for himself. And the dream had
built to a climax of a vision through the dreamer's superconscious,
where he had seen the necessity of making his will one with "that
Element that gave to the forces of the world that necessary . . . to
bring all to the throne of grace." For "He, that gave self as the

ransom, is able to keep that committed unto Him against that [final] day for every individual who puts his trust in Him; for in *Him* comes the way and the light ... [the promise that] I will go, I will meet, I will give that rise of expression in the hearts of men" —the same prayerful "rise unto the throne" which the dreamer had felt in the dream. For the dreamer had, said the Cayce source, experienced a true vision, showing him that "that Spirit is alive in the world today, even as on that glorious morn when He broke the bonds of death and rose in the morning light to the Father." He had actually seen Christ, who "gave all to this world that men, through Him, might seek that way of escape from the fleshly lusts that beset in their various ways"—as just such lusts troubled the dreamer, or those he had seen in states beyond death. There was a way appointed, both before and after death, and such dreams could properly guide the life and the prayers, so that "men—through Him— might be sons and heirs with Him of that [promised] position: Oneness with the Father."

In dream after dream, the Cayce trance source traced the thread of destiny within freedom for people in their groups and institutions. A stock salesman dreamed that he would have his own firm, and saw how he could purchase a seat on the exchange. The reading from Cayce assured him that it would be so, if he kept faithful to his ideals and worked hard. Years later, an associate of the broker dreamed that their business and philanthropic affairs would require them to occupy three floors of an office building on Broadway; Cayce's source explained that the dream was mostly emblematic, but that their activity was along lines set to bring this about—as events proved— in "magnanimous, and enormous space, place and position." Cayce himself dreamed in detail of the construction of the Cayce Hospital at Virginia Beach that he had so long desired, and was assured in readings that it was coming—as four others were assured who dreamed correctly of the same promise, even to details of the building and its medical program.

In 1927 a writer had been pondering how he might present in books and articles the current situation in China, so as to avert coming bloodshed over white exploitation. He had the following dream, in response to his deep concern:

A room in China. Chinese had food and were preventing whites from eating. Some whites seemed to have made money, and I paid off one big tall fellow who had been demanding it. Then I gave back the money. The man paid sought to get out, but was forced out of one exit. As he went out, he said that he hoped to get away alive. I heard music, and they told me it was a death march and indicated that he had been taken. I saw Chinamen fling hungry white men about, who sought the food (ham, it was) for their starving and enslaved selves. 900-299

The reading taken on this dream commented that the dreamer had, by his prayerful concern, conceived an accurate picture, "true in fact," of the situation in China, and had correctly represented in the dream the need of Western reparations for exploitation. His task was then to contribute what he could, through his writing talents, to setting forth the situation.

Dreams could unfold corporate affairs as well as individual, and point the way ahead.

Still other dreams showed the corporate destinies of those who sought the coming of the Lord. Cayce dreamed of groups of people separated where water ran over rocks, and of each group defined by the character of its surroundings. The people sought to catch a fish, which broke, and they tried to put it together again. His reading told him he had seen a depicting of the various religions of the world, needing awakening; the water had been the living water, the living way, which separated each according to his deeds. The fish had been a "representation of Him who became the Living Way, the Water of Life, given for the healing of all the nations." As the fish had been the ancient Christian symbol for Christ, the breaking of the fish had been the division and separation of Christian groups. Yet Cayce could be sure that from God "will there be brought the force that will again make this the Living Way, the perfect representation of the Force necessary to give the life to all." Healing of religious separations was destined by the Father who heard all men's prayers.

Few dreams ever presented to the Cayce source for interpretation had for Cayce and his associates a greater sense of the mysterious timing and initiative of God than the dream had by Cayce himself on September 15, 1931. In it he saw a meeting of the recently formed study groups of friends in the Norfolk area, who would in time produce the little book called *A Search for God.* At the dream meeting one of the members explained that she would inform the group what the next reading was going to tell them to do—namely, to form a circle for healing prayer for the ill. She designated exactly who should be members of the group, and who the leader, as well as the times of day that they should pray together for a list of people—identified in the dream as "the Mohammedan hours of prayer." Cayce even saw the group in the dream preparing for breathing exercises, and for other approaches to their work of healing prayer—which in fact they used in later years.

The reading taken on the dream confirmed the rightness of the details, and the group, called the "Glad Helpers" in Southern church tradition, was formed to practice spiritual healing. The group secured readings on every aspect of healing prayer, over the years which followed, and laid a foundation of activity which continued and grew even after Cayce's death. Most of the original counsel on prayer and meditation in the Cayce materials was given at their initiative; today it awaits systematic research and publication.

The beginning had been made in a dream, calling together a group for a work of "prayer for those who are sick or afflicted in any manner." To the members it was clear that dreams could anchor prayer, call forth prayer, direct prayer—both for individuals and for groups who sought to walk with the Lord of the End.

Individual Destiny in Dreams

Of the many dreams presented to the Cayce source which seemed to that source to contain notes of the divine purposeful action with men, there were even more embodying individual destiny than corporate destiny. Often the note of individual promise was signaled by the appearance of gold in the dream. A young businessman who had spent a year and a half deepening his prayer life, and using his spare time for religious studies had this dream:

> I saw a metal eagle flying over the ocean. The metallic bird soared high and low, sometimes wavering and almost dropping into the water. Finally it landed safely, gliding gracefully though at times waveringly to earth. 900-117

The reading from Cayce assured him that the eagle had been golden, and an "omen, as it were" of the "highest elements of power and might in action," as spiritual forces were awakening him for "a more perfect understanding of those studies as the entity now entering into, see?" As in similar mythopoetic dreams, this was a herald dream, signaling "the first presentation of many" dreams concerning the action of the divine with man, coming to the dreamer—as in fact they did.

His brother, who had joined him in his spiritual pilgrimage, had a comparable dream three months later.

> Saw a woman's face. It was pretty, and had an expression of what appeared to me as "Love," and also a "Gay" and "Free" expression. She pulled a piece of gold-colored cloth up to her chin. She held the cloth there by two sticks, one in each hand, one end of the sticks was cork covered. She was going through the (length of the) gold cloth, holding it by the sticks, one in each hand, up above her head. 137-35

The Cayce reading treated the beautiful woman in that setting as it often did contrasexual figures for dreamers, as representing the guiding, promising force quickening within the dreamer: "in love, in strength, in power, in money, in every force ... through the application of those truths and lessons as are being gained day by day, see?" The gold cloth was a representation of truths about the divine, to be found in the messages of guidance and quickening that would increasingly come to the dreamer in his family life, his business life, his social life, his health, his studies. However, he would need to keep his balance, as was seen in a dream a few nights later:

> A headless man in uniform of a sailor was walking in an erect manner with either a gun or a cane in his hand. 137-36

Here, the gun or cane represented "certain stages of the condition of the body physically, mentally," as it would to Freud represent the proving of manhood, while the uniform and military bearing represented the doing of duty in daily work. The lesson to this ambitious young financier was "Do not lose the head too much in duty as seen, [if it is desired] to accomplish the greater lessons as may be learned from the association of ideas as pertain to things more spiritual." It was a lesson with which the young man would have to grapple often, as the next few years made him a millionaire, in part through his growing psychic ability to guess the activities of stocks.

A man most responsive to beautiful women submitted to Cayce many dreams of girls which were interpreted as rebukes to the dreamer. But then came a dream of promise, again with girls, after three years of a disciplined life of study, service, prayer.

> I beheld beautiful figures of girls, and myself, on a staircase. They said to me: "You are fortunate indeed, for you have been chosen." 900-324

The dreamer had already correctly guessed, said the Cayce source, the meaning of the dream as an assurance that he could go forward in his desire to lecture and to write, for his hard work had made him as one "chosen as the light bearer that may bring much joy, peace, and understanding to many, see?" Within a few months the dreamer was in fact lecturing at the Cayce Hospital which he helped to found, and active in the creation of Atlantic University. But the dreams of the same night contained for him a specific warning of stock market changes, beginning with steel stocks and leading to the 1929 Depression—a development which precipitated crises for the dreamer and the eventual dissolution of both hospital and university.

As one dreamer saw, fulfilling God's destiny for an individual required a strong foundation of faith:

> Saw the huge concrete bridge the C. R. R. of N. J. is building, especially the wonderful $10,000,000 foundation. 900-112

Responding to this dream, the Cayce source warned the dreamer, as always, of the need for a balanced, orderly life, in the "work the body physically and mentally capable of coping with," if set on "a firm and fixed foundation." For "as bridge means way, foundation of the way must be right," for only as every venture were grounded in God might it "be carried through with impunity and with the truth as is necessary."

Equally simple but direct were the dream challenges to a bright and aggressive young man of eighteen.

> Dreamed of riding with someone to the top of a high mountain. Then they showed me a beautiful view spread out below. They said something—recall. 341-15

Obligingly, the Cayce source recalled the rest of the dream. The dreamer had been taken up on the mountain to get "the more perfect understanding of the physical world." At a time when he was deciding on his vocation, and how far to use his brains to acquire possessions, the question had been put to him in the dream, "Though beautiful—and one gain the whole world and lose his own soul, what is the gain therein?" The right perspective was seen in the dream of the next night.

> Dreamed of being picked up by an elephant. May have been more. Recall. 341-15

The Cayce reading spoke of the elephant as representing the intellectual capacities of the boy: "power, might, cunning, with all the mental proclivities of that gained through knowledge." The intent of the dream was that the young man should let himself be "picked up by such wisdom," going on through college, but "studying to show the abilities to use and apply same in the manner as acceptable unto Him"—a Biblical paraphrase. For the rest of the dream had shown the youth rescued from the elephant by the keeper, an emblem of Him who would be able to "keep" what the lad committed to Him throughout his life, taming "worldly knowledge."

A young Jewish man who had begun to study the Bible regularly, as part of his devotional life, had a brief dream in his New York City apartment.

> I was reading Isaiah, that portion where God overcomes those of veneered righteousness but of inner wickedness, hypocrisy, insincerity. I dozed and saw chariots and hand-to-hand battle in which someone, who seemed to be me, was raging, spear in hand. When I awakened, I thought: "Now, as then,

only different methods," and I thought of the haughty Kaiser and his defeat in spite of claiming God on his side—yet in spite of the claim relying not on God's strength of righteousness but on his own physically constructed army. ... The lesson applies today as then ... to each of us. 900-141

The Cayce source explained that the dreamer had experienced a vision based on reading the Bible—showing how Bible study could actually influence dreams. He had glimpsed, as in other dreams of himself as a warrior, how he must temper his own "presented force"—his anger and proneness to self-righteous causes—so that he could make his will one with God's. In such attunement he might dare to touch upon the very same processes which had made Isaiah capable of vision as a prophet , when his "oneness of Spirit with the Father" had given the prophet "the knowledge as is written of him who came into the world" as the Servant. The dream had brought him his peril and his promise.

Many months later the same dreamer saw yet more clearly the destiny and hope of every man who placed his talents wholly at the disposal of God. This dream began, as the Cayce source said such dreams often did, with a review of the dreamer's progress, using scenes from out of his early manhood in Indiana storekeeping, and the promise of an inheritance from his grandmother who owned the stores.

> In Indiana, a store seemed to be for sale, and I told another man of it, and also my uncles of it, giving everybody a fair chance to buy it. I told them the owner had to do with my grandmother's impression ... [as] the voice said, "Now I will give you a half interest in my stores that you so well deserve." I have never felt so gratified by anything as by that "I will give you of mine, because you so well deserve it." I rejoice at deserving anything of and from the Lord. 900-302

At this point in the telling of the dream, the entranced Cayce interrupted to tell the dreamer that he "may well rejoice in the promise," symbolized by an inheritance from his loved and spiritual grandmother. For he was beginning to glimpse the fulfillment of his own true talents and destiny, established from the beginning by God—as "to each individual there is given that spark, that breath, that imprint, that image, of the divine Creative Energy as manifested in material world." What an individual attained in "position, place, station, ability" was determined by his effort to "use and apply" that primal gift of unique capacities given to each soul. How far his destiny reached as a stockbroker—his present vocation—could be seen in the next part of the dream, where the dreamer had a remarkable experience of his potential:

> Thereafter it seemed I could ask any question about stocks that I chose to ask, and it was answered. I stood under a lighted lamp at about dusk. A man walked up and I asked him how U.S. Steel closed. He said, "It closed crazy, at 178."

This part of the dream, said the counseling Cayce, showed the full gifts the dreamer could one day develop. Yet it also disclosed the danger to the dreamer of misinterpreting his stock guidance by fear and doubt, getting out of the Light under which he should stand as in the dream, and producing "crazy" counsel. The dream continued:

> Then the whole market opened up to me.

There followed dream passages in quick sucession on C. and O. railroad stock, on leather stocks, on food stocks—all showing, said Cayce, how clearly the dreamer could receive guidance if he continued to serve others (as he had served the uncles at the start of the dream), and to stand in the Light through his devotional life and commitments. As events followed, the dreamer developed exactly the capacity on the stock market suggested in the dream, and became a millionaire within two years. Most of his guidance during this period came in dreams, augmented by inner promptings on the floor of the stock exchange.

Part of the sense of destiny which could be found in dreams, according to the Cayce source, was the awareness of being helped from beyond oneself. One dreamer heard in his sleep in the early morning:

> Voice: "And when thou art in trouble, or when thou stumblest, I will give my angels charge over thee." And behold my father, and thereafter my mother-in-law [both of them dead] appeared unto me. 900-92

The Cayce source explained that as one was engaged in a worthy work for others, he would indeed draw to himself the aid of "angels in charge," some of whom might be discarnates such as relatives and some of whom might be of very different character. Their helping action might be experienced as in a later part of the dream.

> My dear mother-in-law appeared, but how she appeared! There was nothing indefinite about it. She came in and swept all before her as though she wanted to get to me sure and true. Her features were very pronounced, and I saw her in greater detail than I can, even now, imagine her. Her usual twinkle that she has for me was not there. Her expression was serious. She wore glasses. She said to me sternly, just two words, or I can only remember two. They were, "Such company!"

Interpreting not only the dream but the dreamer, the Cayce source made it clear that this had been a genuine experience of the departed mother-in-law, and intended to warn the dreamer to improve his whole round of associates, both men and women, lest he jeopardize his marriage and his potential for service in his vocation. It was an unpleasant warning for the dreamer, who was often tempted to prove his manhood with women, as well as to brag to his business associates. But he made some changes after the dream.

Again and again the Cayce source insisted that dreamers could see in dreams their great potential in lives spent in "the closer walk" with God. But they would also have to learn that the potential was equaled by responsibility for service, in meekness and lowliness of spirit. A dreamer saw himself several times in dreams as the captain of the great ocean ship, *Leviathan*, and the Cayce source said that the image was not too great to depict his final potential in the next forty years of his life. But some of these same dreams showed him boasting of his captaincy, and the entranced Cayce reminded him that the captain of a ship must operate for the lowliest passenger on board, not just for those at the captain's table. The same dreamer, a man of considerable wealth and position, saw himself as carrying suitcases for his associates who mistook him for a porter; the prayer-attuned Cayce told him he was shown he must be the servant of others—just as in a dream where he lost everything, but received a holy promise:

I had lost most of my worldly possessions. I was occupied in a capacity humble and looked down upon by many. I was disregarded. I was sweeping the dirty, wet sidewalks, trying to get them clean. The subconscious me viewed this physical me with pity. Finishing my task, I took a Sunday newspaper. ... My recreation lay in that Sunday funny-page; it was a frivolous moment of physical relief for the physically struggling mind. 900-226

The Cayce source had shown him, in other dreams of comic pages, how necessary were humor and lightheartedness for those who would "walk the way"' The dreamer continued:

Fast I held to my ideals, trying not to complain, and to manifest the highest and best within me, and to show others, if only they would listen. Then the Voice spoke, and the Lord spake unto me and said: "But come, I will make you a promise. . . . Whilst thou art in the flesh, thou shalt labor and serve all men; but when thou art come into the Spirit, thou shalt be risen unto Me. . . ."

Once again, the note of "coming." The lesson of the dream, said Cayce in his altered state, was the example of "the Master":

He made Himself of low estate, that He might *gain* the more. He made himself abased, that He might bring others to that Light. That is . . . though others may laugh, may scoff, may even consider the entity [the dreamer] simple-minded, vague, uncouth, uncomely, unreasonable, and the light of the physical world may look askance at the efforts of the entity, *God* looketh not on the outward appearance, but upon the heart. For, as is seen in this promise that comes from the infinite to this entity, in the vision [it is] as has been given of old, "Be thou faithful to the end, would thou wear the Crown of Life."

But then the Cayce source warned severely against the inflation which could seize the dreamer with such "a promise from the infinite forces in heaven."

There came unto the Master those that would say: "This request we ask of thee. When thou comest into the kingdom, wilt thou that I sit on thy right hand and my brother on thy left?" And, as the reply, comes, "This is not for *me* to give. But art thou able to drink of that cup that would merit that position? Art thou able to take on those conditions, as would bring full consciousness to that inmost being of yourself, [so] as to make of yourself no estate, that thou mightest serve others?" ... This may be given as the crowning glory of the promises as have been made to the entity from time to time. Then, study these. Ponder these well in thine heart, for the glory of the Lord is ready to be shed abroad ... that others may gain the better knowledge of Him.

So that the dreamer could see that the promises of the Lord were not mere words, he had been given that very night a true vision of something practical. He had been shown the son which would be born to him almost exactly a year from then.

I was in bed and beheld a beautiful golden-haired child. Somebody else was viewing the child with me. "O what a wonderful son to have," I said. "What a beautiful and ideal child. I surely wish God would give me one like that. I want a child." The child climbed into the other person's arms. "Other children are so different," I continued, "so lacking in these wonderful qualities. What a beautiful boy!" Then I beheld [the scene] and heard the voice, both together. Voice: "You will have one child—son." I saw a tall young man, my own son, and he was eating at the table. He was attending college at this age. Voice: "He will be bright, very good in his studies and at college, but will be inclined to be wild. Might get into mischief."

The dreamer's one son was in fact born a beautiful baby, who proved very bright as he grew up. At college age he married another man's wife, and had a nervous breakdown; yet he proved a sensitive, delightful person. The interpretation from the counseling Cayce at the time of the dream was that there had been given both an accurate vision and a symbolic quickening. For the dreamer should also study his own sonship to the divine, the "other person" of the dream who could "control, build up, guide, guard, direct the ways." By preparing his own sonship, the dreamer could best prepare for the right knowledge he could someday give his son.

In the view of the Cayce source, dreamers might find every

aspect of the way prepared for them by the One in whose coming they should rejoice, and to whom they should pray. Even after death there was a destined way, as this woman dreamed of her dead parents.

> Asked Mother if she was with Father, and Mother explained that they were on different planes. And asked if they could communicate. Mother answered, "Of course." 136-78

The Cayce "information" interpreted this dream as one of a series showing the young woman what death was like, and showing her that she could in fact communicate in dreams with her parents, as they with one another—if the contact were made as a result of prayer for them. "For all force is one, and when one applies self and attains through attunement, through that consciousness that may approach [in prayer] the Universal consciousness, then these experiences sought may come through." But one should make no mistake about the state after death; this state would be found to mirror what one had done and been in the present life—as the young woman's husband had seen a year previously, in a dream of his own mother, still living.

> Saw my mother unconscious, and then back in [her home town], dead. It seemed she returned there and died, and people were talking of coming to view the corpse. I said, "My mother was born here. Now she had returned to her birthplace where the Lord has again taken her unto Himself." 900-302

This vivid dream, said the Cayce source, had shown how "All must become as little children, would they enter in." The dreamer must do whatever he could, "so far as lies within the entity's power," to help his mother understand, before she died, this "simple, trusting mind of the child," symbolized by seeing her in the home of her childhood. Only such faith in God would give the mother "insight into the real truth in self, in the application of material or spiritual conditions, for the welfare of self, in body, in mind, in material affairs." For the human being must return to an estate of childlike closeness to God, consciously chosen, if he would fully live in this life or the next. This was human destiny.

Yet the hidden End of man was not best grasped by imagery of other states, other planes, other realms, in the view of the Cayce readings on dreams which could anchor prayer. The picture was better seen as a businessman had, in a dream so important that he was prepared for it by earlier dreams:

> Saw an arrow from a bow. Arrow went powerfully and high.
> 137-35

The intent was a warning to get ready for a spiritual message, said the unconscious Cayce.

Then the message came, in a dream where Christ himself was seen. He came toward the dreamer as the Man who could disclose others as hardly distinguishable from Himself.

> A man approached many, including myself, in what seemed to be a hotel lobby. When he first approached us, he had the appearance of a detective, but as he drew near I had the feeling that he was Jesus Christ. 137-50

Here the dreamer, said the prayer-attuned Cayce, had seen how "in groups, in the individual, in the mass, even" there could be found "in the form of man, as man to man" the coming of the redeeming Force from on high, not as detective or policeman or judge to condemn man, but as the Unknown Christ. When the dreamer sought to build his whole life around such spiritual forces, he would begin to discover what "the Christ's coming means to the whole world." He, the Lord of the Coming and of the End, sought in prayer, might be found in a hotel lobby, illuminating the face of the next man met, if one would but look.

CHAPTER 5

The Kingdom of God
Is at Hand:
Mystical Dreams

The second phase of Jesus' saying comes right to the point: "The Kingdom of God is at hand." Something is astir, as close as hands and pulsing wrists, nearer than breathing.

The modern mind, trained in centuries of Greek subject-object dichotomy, hears this claim as the description of an order, an arrangement. Perhaps it is a subjective arrangement, a warm, sincere confidence within, or an enviable peace of mind and soul. Perhaps it is an objective arrangement, a just and durable social order, or a Pax Christi that may someday become the Pax Romana as well.

But Jesus was a Jew, not a Greek. He came from a tradition that produced neither speculative philosophers nor empire. He came from a people steeped not in systems and arrangements, but in living covenants between persons present. His Kingdom was the reign of Somebody, not merely a state of affairs. It was the doing of the Ancient of Days, of the Nameless One who had told Moses, "I will be there as I will be there." He spoke of a Presence.

As the eschatological dimension of faith sees God at work in time, fashioning destinies within freedom that may only be guessed until man stands at the End, so the affirmation of the Reigning Presence evokes the mystical dimension of faith. Where the other phrase suggests "Something can happen," this one suggests "Someone is here!"

It fell to Jesus to prod men, lure them, offend them, heal them, accost them, until at last something melted far within them, and they could suck in their breaths to stammer, "Someone *is* here!" He had to use spatial imagery of a kingdom "in heaven" and yet "within," but he had also to transcend spatial imagery, until God was no longer localized as up or down, out or in—but present, present. To such a God his hearers might pray, "Hallowed be Thy Name!"

Jesus' own vivid sense of the Presence was to be seen not alone in the overshadowing that had fallen upon him as he stood in the baptismal waters; it would be seen in that moment when he lost it, crying out, "Why hast thou forsaken me?"

On the one hand, the Presence in all ages appears to be felt as companionship, as the giving of no less than the real being of a Father, who calls each one by name. It is apprehended as the dizzying gift of One who pays the late laborers as much as the first, whose ways are love unspeakable, drink without price, absurd Grace.

On the other hand, the Presence appears to be felt as urgent love —that love which Rudolf Otto has described as "God's quenched wrath." The Presence is love which burns with truth, which transforms and purifies whom He chooses, which calls men to action now for others.

As the prayer response to the Lord of the Eschaton tends to be *obedience*, so the prayer response to the Presence tends to be *being*. "Let me so love!" "Forgive us!" "Lord, remember me when Thou comest into Thy kingdom!" Or, if the heart fails, "Woe is me!" "Depart from me!" The praying person responds with a leap of longing to be alive, to be aware, to be truthful, to stand firm and single of heart before the Face. Yet even as he does so, he finds his cup overflowing, and he hurries to spread a table for his enemies, not alone for his friends.

The Cayce readings insisted that the Presence offered to man was real, not poetic or "merely religious." Every man could, through prayer and meditation, come to know God, not simply know of Him. One person asked in a reading, "Why is it that at times my meditation seems unsatisfactory?" The answer from the Cayce source led up to the promise of the Presence.

> Ye are still in the flesh. Why did He [say], "Father, why hast thou forsaken me?" Even when the world was being over-come, the flesh continued to rebel. For "When I would do good, evil is present with me" [as the Scripture says]. But, "Though I take the wings and fly to the utmost parts of the heavens, Thou art there; though I make my bed in hell, Thou art there."

> So, when doubt and fear come, close thy sense to the material things, and lose thyself in Him. Not that ye shall not be joyous in the things that partake of the pleasures, even of life; for so did He. But keep thy consciousness ever alert, ready and willing to be the channel that will make known His love. And He will speak with thee! 281-3

To one woman the Cayce source spoke earnestly of the Presence, in terms often used in the Cayce readings.

> There is that access, then, that way to the Throne of grace, of mercy, of peace, of understanding, within thine own self. For He has promised to meet thee in thine own temple, in thine own body, through thine own mind.

> And as He has given of old, as He has made manifest in the flesh, as He has spoken to thee and to thy fellow man again and again: consecrate your mind, your body. Purge same in a manner that to thee in thine own consciousness has made, and does make, thee as receiving the Lord, thy God! And then enter into the holy of holies, within thine own conscious-ness. Turn within; see what has prompted thee. And He has promised to meet thee there.

> And there it shall be told thee, from within, the steps thou shouldst take day by day, step by step. Not that some great exploit, some great manner of change should come within thine body, thine mind. But line upon line, precept upon

precept, here a little, there a little. For it is, as He has given, not the knowledge alone but the practical application in thy daily experience with thy fellow man that counts. Not that one seeks out this, that, or the other manner or channel [of wonders]. For lo, He is within thine own self—yet without —that He may guide, guard, direct thy ways day by day.

She wondered why she was not making better progress. "Why do I not make a more continuous effort?" The response was also a question.

Is thy purpose a single one? Or art thou seeking, seeking, without putting into practice that thou knowest?

She would have to begin in the little things, the reading continued.

Studying to show thyself approved unto Him. Not as an eye servant—but as ye do it unto those that ye meet, as ye do it unto those in thine own house, as ye do it unto those that ye meet day by day. A smile, a cheery word, a hopefulness, optimistic ever—in Him. For He is the way, He is the abundant supply, if ye but put thy trust in Him.

At the same time, she could pray.

Enter into thine inner chamber with thy Lord. Meet Him there; seek and ye shall know. For He would speak with thee as thou wouldst with thy child. As thou, as a mother, lovest that which is of thee, of thine own body, of thine own blood, then knowest thou not—as thou wouldst be gentle, as thou wouldst be patient, thy heavenly Father would be more patient with thee? Trust in Him; speak oft with Him! 992-1

If dreams can in fact function to anchor prayer, then a second dimension of dream action would be to quicken exactly this sense of the Presence to which the Cayce source referred. However the waking mind might stumble over the problem of conceiving the One in His immediacy, dreams might lead the sleeping mind directly to Him whom Jesus said was "at hand."

Brought to the Presence, by whatever dream imagery, the dreamer might find the mystical dimension of his prayer life more secure, and might respond with the longing to come alive which so often marks the mystical prayer.

The promise of a dream Presence was in the counsel of the Cayce source to a music teacher.

> Then, as the physical consciousness is laid aside, there may come dreams or visions, and even He, the Lord, the Brother, may show thee. For He is the same yesterday, today, and forever. And He hath promised to speak with thee, if ye desire same—possibly in dreams, in visions, or in the still small voice within. 1992-1

Cayce himself had a delightful dream that made a point to him by referring to the New Testament incidents of Jesus' feeding the multitude with loaves and fishes. The dream opened with the Duke and Duchess of Windsor, who had appeared in other dreams of Cayce's as symbols of success and respectability—as well as of the money which Cayce lacked at the time of this dream in 1937, as so often in his life.

> Jesus and I, with the Duke of Windsor and his wife, were at a large gathering—seemed in Paris.

> We came to a place where drinks were being served out on the sidewalk, under a canopy. I said, "Let's have a drink." We four sat down and all ordered champagne. I wondered why I had done that, for I realized I only had three cents in my pocket. When we got up, the Duke and his wife walked away. Jesus and I were standing there—I searched my pockets and brought out the three cents. Jesus threw his head back and laughed aloud, clapped his hands together, and said, "Will I have to send you after a fish, too?"

It was the kind of dream that could take away much fear about money, before an unforgettable Face.

Five years before, just after he had lost his hospital and university, Cayce had reported a dream which seemed intended to establish a Presence stronger than fear and doubt.

> I visioned God, and He promised that He wouldn't turn His face away.

The reading taken on this little dream said it had indeed been a vision. The promise had been one that Cayce needed "while going through that period of transition, in the material sense"; it was the assurance "as of old" that "if ye will be my people, I will be your God." Then, within a few weeks, there came to Cayce a memorable quickening.

> While meditating in afternoon, the same exuberant feeling came over me that used to years ago, but which had been lost to me for twenty-five years.

The reading taken on this experience told Cayce his inner self was awakening to new potentials, through his meditation and the "higher forces" accompanying meditation. After this time, Cayce would have heightened abilities, as would a number of others. "As has been given, 'Your young men shall dream dreams, your old men shall see visions, your maidens shall prophesy.' These are coming to pass, with the upheavals as are just before the world in many a quarter!" It was the same kind of assurance which Cayce reported in a waking experience.

> While in church, the words in the song book spoke to me and danced right before my eyes. The words, "My grace is sufficient for thee," seemed to be impressed upon me.

His trance source told him simply that it had been an experience best described in a Biblical paraphrase: "My words shall go before you, will ye seek Me while I may be found!"

Like Cayce, others were experiencing a Presence outside of dreams as well as in dreams. To one person working on dreams and prayer the sense of the divine came with the sense of the present reality of someone he loved who had died.

> In the afternoon, while praying, and in that part of the prayer asking forgiveness of a relative who is gone. A definite impression of an arm coming about my shoulder and pressing the shoulder. When the impression became so distinct as to even move the shirt sleeve, I foolishly jumped up in fright. Yet even as I did, I thanked Him for coming to me in that hour of need. 900-256

The entranced Cayce explained that the dreamer had actually experienced communication, through the barrier of death, brought about "in the supplication of prayer, or attunement with that divine force of that [promise] as has been given, 'My Spirit beareth witness with thy spirit whether ye be the sons of God or not.' " The dreamer should not be afraid, whether these experiences came to him awake or asleep, if he made "self at one with His desires, His ambitions, being in that direction of giving to others that fuller concept of the Christ life in the earth today"; he was experiencing "more and more those beauties of those who love the Lord and His appearing."

Often the Cayce "information" instructed dreamers to pay attention to a certain kind of voice that might address them in dreams or awake. Such a voice was reported by a young stockbroker in this experience.

> While reading the crucifixion of Christ in the Bible. Voice gently called my name. 900-170

Speaking in his altered state, the tuned-in Cayce told him that this had been an experience similar to that of Samuel of old, to which the man of today should also respond, "Here am I, Lord. Use me!" This was ever the prayerful answer to the real Presence. In the present dream the call had come to direct the dreamer's whole being to a better understanding of sacrifice. As a stockbroker, the dreamer had recently made a mistake and lost much money on Atlantic Gulf stock. At that time, too, he had heard the voice.

> The voice said, "Atlantic Gulf," and at the same time I saw the outline of the face of Christ, together with what seemed to be a guiding star or light.

The Cayce source patiently explained that in the times of Christ, as at present in the dreamer's life, adversity and persecution had brought men greater spiritual growth than had success and popularity. But if the dreamer would study the full cycle of the crucifixion and the resurrection, it would bring to his consciousness a better sense of the cycles of stocks, even to a practical change in Atlantic Gulf stocks again, soon. It would "come very suddenly, as the advance and the decline comes steadily in the Life of which we have now been using [the image] as a physical concept of same, see?" There was only one helpful Force at work in the universe,

seen in the life and presence of Christ and in the perceiving of the
movement of stocks, when the purpose was "service, service, service."

A woman in a study group asked about her dream of a Presence.

> Please give me the significance of the dream I had the night
> of September 26th, at which time I saw the Master. 262-55

Commenting on her dream from his altered state, Cayce assured
her she had received a confirmation of her purpose and thought and
activity of recent months. She should not be afraid, but "rather
know that self is being led by Him who *is* the Guide, the Giver,
the Promise to all mankind." In dreams one might meet More than
oneself.

Dreams of the Presence with Nature

As the Cayce source pointed out the sense of the divine as a present
Reality coming in dreams, it touched upon the dream content of
Nature, of created forms, and of persons.

The quickening felt in dream scenes of Nature was usually not
difficult for the dreamer to understand. One grown man felt it in
both a scene from childhood and a scene of unknown beauty.

> As a child I used to love to roam in reverie through Central
> Park, particularly in Spring, Summer and Fall. I found much
> peace in these quiet periods of reflection and dreams of the
> imagination. I saw myself [in a recent dream] doing that
> again, with a lovely house or home in some country as my
> goal.

The reading on the dream suggested that the dreamer had gone
back to childhood scenes out of doors to recapture "the meditations
of the entity in those days when the inner consciousness of the
entity builded in the mental forces those conditions as would bring
the great joy, peace and happiness." As often, a dream of return to
early scenes was intended to stir up the values quickened in just
those places. But the part of the dream that followed contained a
threat.

Suddenly a change from warmth and sunshine to cold, snow, and ice. I found myself on a thawing lake—the ice mighty thin and dangerous. I became frightened, turned back, and had a narrow escape from sinking through the thin ice. As I reached safety, that lovely house and its peaceful surroundings entered my mind, and the voice of a girl said: "I'll go on painting and preparing the house just the same." 900-205

Here, the reading indicated, the dreamer was seeing what happened when he became afraid, losing trust in the spiritual forces he had been building into his life. But the girl who spoke was, as other lovely women he had sometimes seen in beautiful surroundings in his dreams, "the voice of the messenger, the truth," assuring him that she would go on building, preparing. He had seen in the house an emblem of what his own mind built for itself, out of materials given to it, out of what the dreamer chose to trust and dwell upon. His inner consciousness could either build on truth or on fear— which was thin ice.

Cayce's wife, Gertrude, was a person who loved natural beauty, as many of her dreams showed. She reported this dream sequence.

Dreams regarding gathering of shells from ocean, seeing various kinds of fish, various people, etc.

The reading on the dream pointed out that while common usage spoke of Mother Earth, "instead of being Mother Earth, it's Mother Sea, see?" For all life had originally come from the sea, and the symbol-making part of dreamers used the sea to represent life itself, and what it brought forth. In this case the dreamer had been shown shells from the sea to stand for people brought to her in the flow of her life: "some are beautiful, some are broken, some are of the various ways and manners, yet that from which they come is of the One Source, see?" She was being shown how to take those who came from all walks of life to ask her husband's help, and to make each one special and beautiful, as far as she could. As she had seen in the dream, she could help each to find his own worth, "as the isle of the sea, with all the beauties that surround same in the earthly sphere, see?" The beauty she treasured in shells she must seek in people, however broken, for they came from the same Source, and were precious to the One Presence.

A businessman reported an odd set of dream images. First there was one in which he saw himself as "playing golf." Commenting, the entranced Cayce told him that golf would be excellent for his physical and mental balance—adding that there was a very good golf course at the place where the dreamer was thinking of spending the summer (a place where Cayce had never been!). But there was more to the challenge, as the next dream fragment showed:

Struck by lightning under tree, and prayer. 900-79

In this scene, the counseling Cayce told him, he was being shown that being out of doors would be good for him spiritually as well as mentally and physically," for the lightning, associated with prayer, exemplified "the higher forces" which could become "the life giving flow." He would find it easier to pray with more of Nature in his life.

The Presence with Nature, inviting men to be true to their own nature, was a theme often emphasized in the Cayce materials, as in these comments made to one person encouraged to work with flowers:

Flowers should be the companions of the lonely. They can bring color again to the cheeks of those who are ill. They can bring to the bride the hope of love, of beauty, of a home. Flowers love places where there is peace and rest. Why do not people learn lessons from the flowers, and grow in love and beauty, whatever may be their environment? Wherever a flower is found, whether in an open field or in a bog, it is beautiful. Why do not people also learn from the flowers that wherever they are, they have the power to make that place beautiful, whether it is a hovel, or a home of the mighty? 5122-L-1

Dreams of the Presence with Forms

Even as Nature could signify the Presence in dreams, and in waking life, so could the various forms which man created—if man let them do so. Music, in the view of the Cayce readings, could be used to arouse either constructive or destructive forces in the psyche, and one must choose what he intended with his music. "For there is a way that seemeth right to man, but the end thereof taketh hold upon hell. As to the experiences that arise from music, choose that which is constructive in the experiences, and know it must partake of that which brings peace to the soul, and not the gratifying of body—or of the emotions of the body—only." This reading continued:

> Music may arouse violent passion, soothe the beast of passion. Music may make for thoughts of home, heaven, or loved ones; the laugh of a baby, the tears of a beautiful woman, the arms of a loved one, the jeers of a crowd . . . 5253-1

So it was with all the arts, which could often be found in such dream material as the hearing of orchestras. But the divine would also be found in the pursuit of truth. One male dreamer reported:

> Girl friend, angel-like, descending [the stairs]. Others didn't see her. 900-54

The Cayce source interpreted this dream as representing "knowledge from superconscious conditions" which was coming to the dreamer out of his studies and prayer life—truth regarding many things both practical and ultimate, "yet unknown, unthought of, unheralded, undesired by many of the ones that should seek out to understand and know just this knowledge." But truth was a demanding lover. Because the dreamer was married, there was also in the vision the hint of disapproval from others over his association with the girl—and the warning echoed by the Cayce source that he should do nothing with the truths and guidance he reached to bring reproach on himself. He should not give up the desire for knowledge, represented by his regard for the beautiful girl, but should use it well. "Cast not aside that desire for knowledge, but seek to give the clearer understanding to those who seek for that City without foundations, whose builder and maker is God." In that way the knowledge, the forms of wisdom, could become for him as a helping angel, rather than as a temptation.

Religious forms, too, had their place in awakening the sense of the divine Presence, as a young Jewish woman saw in this dream.

Saw my mother-in-law in Temple. 136-8

To the Cayce source, the Jewish temple for this woman stood as "representing the spiritual element that enters into the conscious forces, in the development of the mental toward any given subject." As the young woman was setting out to study psychic development for herself, she would need to "harken often unto those precepts as would come to the body through these forces, in the same manner and way as if those precepts were given through the temple worship."She would soon need to learn about inner spiritual guidance; when it came, she must take it as seriously as corporate public worship, where the Ark and the Torah had meant so much to her since girlhood.

But not every religious form, thought, rite, or institution was equally effective in mediating the Presence, as one dreamer saw in this scene.

> Was seated in a sort of grandstand seat on the beach, and another man sat next to me. We looked out to sea, and there, close to the beach, was what seemed the hulk of a wrecked boat, rising and lowering in the sea. "It is now coming mighty close to land and to us," I said to my companion. "Yes," he nodded, "they can't pump the water out of that!" Up and down, up and down, rising and lowering with the waves, rose and fell this monster; and nearer and nearer it came to us, until it was almost on top of us and I could see the water filling up and rushing out of the holes in the side.
>
> Then the monster hulk, that appeared as a drifted wrecked ship, seemed up on the beach, still rising and falling, the water filling it up and rushing out of it again. I wondered why they didn't pump all the water out, and again the other man said, "They can't do it—they can't pump the water out of that!"
>
> Then I ran up this monster, still rising and falling, filling and emptying with water, and I noticed the old wooden step affair of the body, and how the water would act to deteriorate and disintegrate those wooden steps. ... 900-102

The Cayce reading on this dream was incisive. The dreamer had seen "the truth in religious thought" in his times as the monster ship adrift, and bearing down upon others in no uncertain manner."

As the thought of pumping out from within had shown, religious thought "might be made whole by action from within, yet this seems inaccessible to many." The dreamer's prompting to go on board was his desire to be helpful, and showed to him the "assistance and aid to such conditions" that he could render, provided that he remembered about the steps—for sensible and graded "stepping stones to the new thought must be made safe and secure for all." Not every form mediated the Presence. Some forms needed cleansing from within, by the action of prayer before the Lord of sea and air, the Lord of water and the spirit.

There were times when the divine would be found in relation to the forms of business, as one Wall Street broker vividly saw.

> Our maid came in and said, "You should be close to the front door, for God may come in. He will enter that way."

The Cayce source reminded that it is ever the servant who can show the way. The dream continued.

> My brother and mother paid little attention to her, but I perked up at once and started forward. And then the maid announced the distinguished visitor, that "God" was calling on us.

> I rushed out into the hall and towards the door. Halfway to the door I met God, and jumped for Him, throwing my arms about His neck, and hugging Him. He embraced me.

It was a scene like that in the parable of the Prodigal Son.

> After that I noticed God's appearance. He was a tall, well-built man, clean cut and clean shaven, wearing a brown suit and carrying a gray derby hat. He had an intelligent look, an eye that was kindly but piercing. He had an expression that was firm and features clean cut. He was very healthy, robust, businesslike, and thorough, yet kindly, just, and sincere. Nothing slouching, shuffling, maudlin, sentimental about Him—a man we might say we'd like to do business with. He was God in the flesh of today, a business or industrial man, not a clergyman, not dressed in black, not a weakling; a strong healthy, intelligent Man, whom I recognized as the Man of today, and whom I welcomed and was glad to see. I recog-

nized in this fine upright Man—not the ordinary—but God.

Here, said the entranced Cayce, the dreamer was being shown in a true vision how God sought man to be equal with Himself—just as the dream had indicated by making God a man, and God Himself had indicated by sending His Son as a man. Next in the dream, as always when man meets God, there came the question of repentance. This was Prohibition time.

> Then we passed my liquor closet. It was half open. God looked in; I showed Him the half-opened closet. But, I thought, I forget He is not the ordinary Man he looks, but God and knows all, so I might as well show Him all, as pretend anything. So I opened the closet wide for Him to see. I showed Him my liquor, particularly the gin which I used for cocktails. "In case of sickness," I said to God. "You are well prepared," God said sarcastically.

Evidently the divine which this dreamer knew was not without humor, even at the time of a man's open confession.

> We proceeded into the parlor where the radio was playing, and my brother and mother amusing themselves with it. I wanted them to meet God, but they couldn't seem to recognize Him. "Of course they would not know Him," I thought. How could they recognize Him, when they have not the faith that He did appear in the flesh *again* in just such a Man as was before me? If they don't *understand* how God appeared in the flesh Christ, how would they recognize a flesh God today? How could they understand that the true manifestation of the true perfection, within, constituted the manifestation of God, whether of a man in one capacity or another?

The prayer-entranced Cayce spoke here with vigor and excitement, telling the dreamer he had caught the full sense of what God had intended when He said, "We will make Man in our own image." For man had been created "to become as God, and One with Him, even as the Son of Man in flesh appeared in the world and made Himself One with man—yet His will, His force, His supply coming from the All Powerful Force." But those who did not take thought, did not pray and meditate, did not take time for "quiet introspection," would ever miss "the God that is presenting Self to man in everyday walks of life."

So they did not see, or at least pay any attention to Him. I sat down on the sofa to converse with Him. "You could work harder," He said.

This was, said the unconscious Cayce, the God who "is the Rewarder of those who diligently seek Him," in business as in everything else, where He pours out His gifts and concern upon men "as the natural consequence of the love of the Father for His creatures," and for "His portion, that would be One with Him."

I almost started to reply, yet bethought me that God knew all —no use. I meekly assented. "You could hardly do less," He continued. "How did you make out in Hup Motors?" I couldn't just say—not so well it seemed. "That is an L. [agency] purchase, an L. recommendation, isn't it?", asked God. I knew that God knew before the asking. "Yes," I replied. "About all you have been doing lately is lifting capital, isn't it?", said God, motioning with His thumb towards my mother [the source of a recent loan]. "Just about," I assented. God looked toward the radio. I was standing, studying the radio, as God disappeared. 900-231

The radio stood for prayer, and for a prayerful life, said the Cayce source. For as "the waves of the air may transmit from one individual to another the things, the conditions, the good, the bad . . . how much more through the infinite forces must the cry, the pleading of every individual, come up to the Father on High!" Each must know "that when they are in attune with the Infinite, how great must be that power which is set in motion to bring about the manifestations of the divine that is within." The radio was an emblem, too, of God's answering response to man, "of the great love that is shown, of the great force and power as is manifested . . . of the great good as may be seen—as even through those weaknesses, or that . . . considered as of sin." In the midst of human frailty and failure, symbolized by the illegal liquor and the indifferent relatives, still, as truly as men are surrounded by airwaves, so—concluded the Cayce source—"in Him we live and move and have our being."

God would make Himself known, as of old, in the midst of the forms of the present, including a business suit and counsel on stock.

Dreams of the Presence with Persons

A man who was warmly responsive to beautiful women reported to the Cayce trance source a brief dream experience:

Felt a hand on my face. 137-35

He was told that as an affectionate person, he would need to be the master of what was called up in his relations with women "and not mastered by same." For his growth, he could find his clue in the image of the disciple, "the beloved who leaned on the Master's breast." There was a way to find the Presence in the most intimate relationships, for "spiritual force in the physical world" might be found by him who sought it to be "as real ... the rise and setting of the sun to the physical eye."

A man who dreamed that his father was ill and needed his care was told that relating to the Father was the first duty of every soul; his dream had come to signify and awaken that relationship, out of the perspective of love for his parent. A woman whose husband's gifts overshadowed hers dreamed that she was running with a man who seemed perfect in every way. The Cayce source told her who that Man was, and reminded her to run with Him, so that she could help her husband rather than demand he be divine.

A hard-boiled businessman, skeptical of the spiritual values held by his father, who had recently died, dreamed the exact details of his father's death.

I saw my father as he was on his death bed, and saw the following that actually occurred just before his death. The rabbi came in and said to my father, "You are not afraid to die, are you?" He answered, "No, I am not afraid, but I want to be with my family always." It occurred to me that it was his creed to always be good to people while they are alive. 137-43

The Cayce reading explained to him that he had in his dream entered "the superconscious state," where he had made a full attunement with the present consciousness of the father, not just with his memory. If the dreamer would ponder the force of what had been shown him, would weigh what he had felt so deeply, in the dream, about his father's creed, he would find the basis for building his own true values before God, "for the fuller, greater development." The Presence could be a gift from the dead to the living, when the dead had really lived.

But it was the dream of an earnest young man, full of the zeal and hope of his religious studies, which caught with special clarity the sense of promise of the Presence, even in a grocery store.

> It seemed I traveled to a place by boat, and there beheld the Master, Christ Jesus. I shouted to all about me as loud as I could: "We can be as He—I have proved it!" None would listen or believe me.

> I entered what seemed to be a grocery store, and there beheld a man who appeared as Christ—it may or may not have been He, but He was dressed as Christ would have been, but younger. A woman said to me: "Isn't He a wonderful God?" "You can be as He," I answered her. "Oh," she replied, "you are not like Him. You are a soft, mushy human." I turned to show her Christ, and it may have been His picture on a box [which] I showed her, but there He was, as I knew Him from pictures I had seen—an older man, sympathetic, yet unyielding in His faith in the Truth, its adherence, and propagation to His fellowman.

> I went up to the store counter and sat down. And there, behind the counter, I saw the younger man like Christ, kneeling down in prayer. He was thanking His Father for much. . . . 900-114

The dream had come, said the Cayce source, to reassure the student that "those who would seek Him, the Master, may find Him." Yet the way to help others find Him would not be in merely proclaiming the truth, showing pictures—even of the central and life-giving truth, the heart of the Good News, "We can be as He!" The dream had shown the rest of the way: "Oft in prayer, even as the Master —oft in communication, then, with Him—will strength and endurance in body, soul and mind come—to him who has viewed a message from Him." A message from Him—this was how dreams could finally anchor prayer, today as truly as in ancient times.

PART THREE

How Dreams
Can Advance Prayer

CHAPTER 6

Repent:
Dreams of Sin
and Redemption

The third part of Jesus' message is the blunt word, "Repent!"

The word strikes modern ears with psychological overtones. It suggests feelings, the proper blend of remorse, regret, confession, abreaction, self-acceptance, and dedication to true genitality and productivity.

But the Hebrew term translated "Repent!" is *teshuvah*, turning. Such turning is not feelings, not one more interesting experience, not a technique of adjustment at all. It is turning of a man's whole being, turning so primal and total that it cannot be depicted in pastels of emotion and adjustment-imagery. It is no less than turning toward God.

Jesus did not appear to offer repentance as a once-for-all remedy for the human condition. In fact, he linked it with a call to believe the good news of God's Grace—such trusting as might be won only in many beginnings, many turnings. But he offered repentance as a starting point. He taught it as a call for forgiveness and a turning from evil, in every day's prayer.

What is the prayer response that embodies repentance? "Thine is the kingdom, the power, the glory!" "I give thee back the life I owe!" It is at least *release*, turning to God and relinquishing the tight grip on one's affairs. Not passive release, a collapsing into the arms of a superparent, but active turning to work in the vineyard with the Father. "Others may do as they may, but as for me and my house, we will serve the living God"—until we lose Him again and must repent anew.

In the view of the Cayce readings, it was never too late for repentance.

> Will is the greater factor, for it may overcome any or all [obstacles], provided the will is made one with the Pattern, see? No influence of heredity, environment, or what-not surpasses the will. Else why would that Pattern have been shown in which the individual soul—no matter how far astray it may have gone—may enter with Him into the Holy of Holies? 5749-14

> It is never too late to mend thy ways. 5248-1

> Be not faint-hearted because failure seems to be in thy way, or that self falters. But—"How many times shall I forgive— or ask forgiveness—seven times?" Yea, seventy times seven! Or—not how I faltered, but did I seek His face again?

> "Could ye not watch with me one hour?"—the Man, crying out. "Sleep on, now, and take thy rest, for the hour cometh when I shall be even alone." So we find the changes, the weaknesses in the flesh.

> Yet he that seeks shall find, and as oft as ye knock will the answer come. Seek to be one with Him, in body, in mind, in soul! 281-7

A total turning, a total repentance would involve more than tinkering with attitudes; it would involve body, mind, soul—action, desire, trust. It would involve prayer that grows, changes, advances, to pace the repentance.

Can dreams advance prayer, by fostering specific turnings? If so, dreams would not only mirror the dreamer's weaknesses, as

Freud so carefully showed, beginning with his own revealing dream of "Irma's injection." Dreams that contributed to prayer would set weaknesses in a perspective that would show God's redemptive work and aid, available to the dreamer.

Such dreams were frequently traced in the Cayce readings. There were dreams that advanced repentance by turning the dreamer's face toward God, rather than freezing his prayer-time gaze on his own real evil. There were dreams that advanced repentance by using such vivid God-with-man imagery as to shock the dreamer into praying to turn here and now. And there were dreams that advanced repentance by linking the dreamer's own prayerful hope of turning Godward with the hope of turning and growth which he gave to others.

Dreams of Turning toward Life

The popular view of repentance sees it as a turning from evil. But there is danger in repentance. Focus on the evil to be avoided, rather than on God who makes all things new, may lead to fascination with evil, even to secret pride in sin. One individual was told to focus on no less than His glory—exactly as the Lord's Prayer handles repentance.

> For what is bad? Good gone wrong, or something else? It is good misapplied, misconstrued, or used in a *selfish* manner . . . for the satisfying of a desire within self.

> And so is sin, so is illness—a lack of at-onement with a coordinant, cooperative Force of a living influence that may . . . become such a marvelous force for good, for a channel of manifestation of good. . . .

> The Lord is willing. Art thou, then, willing to accept and be guided, and be directed, by that Influence in thy experience?

> How, then, would ye seek to know?

> For thou art [often] not in error, but rather in the slough of doubt, of fear. And as the mental self seeks to justify its activity in any direction . . . and seeks excuses—what is thine? That thou art not understood, or that others do not understand? Why? Hast thou told it to Jesus? He knows; He under-

stands! And if He understands, then what care ye? Or dost thou consider what others think, rather than what He may give thee day by day?

In thy material applications, seek ye first the Lord while He may be found!

For He is above price . . . whether of body, of mind, or even purse. But know that thou art His and He is thine, and that He beareth witness with *thee*! Not only in what ye think, but in that that ye do to thy fellow man, they neighbor . . . yea, to thy foe! To those that despitefully use you, that say all manner of hard things about you! Did they not the same about Him?

Ye say, "This is generality . . . and not to me, but to anyone." Behind what are ye hiding? Thine own conceit, that you are different? No different from any other soul, seeking . . . .

And if thou art found worthy, thou mayest occupy even a seat of glory. For thou wilt make thy body, thy mind, a means, a way, an expression of His glory! 1089-MS-1

A dreamer preoccupied with how to reach unbelievers had a pert dream which invited him to turn fully into the direction of his best work, rather than worry about luring others into agreement with him.

I was walking along the street; noticed a girl with particularly short dresses, and nice form. Despite her rather vulgar display, she seemed to have a strict sense of propriety. A taxicab came along and wanted to go one way and she shook her head, making him turn around to the way she pointed. "We are going that way," she said. 900-91

Commenting on the woman "who seems to present more of charms than necessary," the Cayce source likened her display to the dreamer's tendency to "proclaiming findings," rather than taking firm steps to "direct self," which alone would reach "those who desire and are seeking." Direction of one's life before the Face was the beginning of repentance.

A similar emphasis was given by the Cayce "information" in response to a small dream by Edgar Cayce, who often found himself surrounded by attractive women fascinated by him. He reported, "Dreamed of talking with King Solomon." His reading on the dream mentioned "the weaknesses of the flesh as were in that entity"—Solomon with his many wives. Yet it urged Cayce to put his effort, even his prayer "attunement," not simply on avoiding problems with women, but on seeking the wisdom of Solomon, "of whom it has been said, 'None that shall rise that in physical [body] will be mightier in wisdom than he.' "

A young student dreamed a nightmare that showed him repentance was more than proclaiming high ideals.

> We were watching a dirigible and an airship that were sailing above us but seemed to be in great distress. Suddenly the dirigible spun on its nose and crashed to the ground in the lawn. I heard the cries and groans of the occupants as the ship struck. The other two people and I started towards the wreck, but were at first warned back by those who survived. A little later we were called on to help carry the injured ones to the house. The man I carried seemed to have hurt his leg, and was crying not take his leg off. Later it seemed that I was again at the wreck. I drank something from a bottle, and then continued to collect tools, a hammer and other things. 341-13

Commenting on the dream, the hypnotized Cayce identified the dirigible and plane as high ideals that could fall and become destructive to the guilty dreamer, requiring drastic self-amputation, if not supported by stability and "strength of character." The right approach was to turn about, and help himself by helping others, even as he had done in the dream. The bottle contained the water of life, ready to assist anyone who chose "that straight and narrow way," and the tools were the "necessary paraphernalia" for his lifework. Not fear of failure and accident, but steadiness of purpose was the repentance needed.

A businessman received several warning dreams, including the following graphic scene that challenged him to choose the level and quality of his life.

> It seemed there were two ways of crossing a river, the upper bridge and the lower. As some others used the lower one, so did I, but this time was lying down and traveling right along

> the water's edge. It seemed dangerous to me, yet had done
> so often before [that] I had full confidence. 900-64

The attuned Cayce responded briefly and pointedly. The river was
the way of life, while the bridge was "the existence, or span
through or over which the material man passes in the passage
through earth's plane." The higher bridge offered "the great, broad
outlook over the whole of Universal Forces," while the lower
bridge was "ever the way of the great masses." The dreamer could
travel on his belly if he chose, and make some progress. But he
knew the right direction in which to turn. The quiet voice of Cayce
closed the reading with a quote from Moses on Mt. Nebo, so often
used in the Cayce materials: "Choose thou, as to whom thou wilt
serve."

But when the same dreamer lost a great deal of money some
months later, on an error in business judgment, he had a dream that
indicated what Cayce's source often counseled: it was better to
continue taking risks than to do nothing. The Cayce "information"
often indicated that it was better to do something wrong with one's
life, than to hold back, for God could correct a life in motion, while
He could do little with one frozen. Here was the dream:

> Saw a train, and I was going on a journey somewhere.
> Seemed to be some reference to my being vaccinated. 900-110

The Cayce trance source spoke of the journey as "the necessity of
movement of self in body, mind, soul," adding that "there is no
standing still." While it was appropriate to take times of quiet,
fulfilling the old injunction, "Be still and hear what the Lord hath
to say," such pausing should not be a freezing from fear. For even
in making mistakes, one had to live and act as though on a journey
or adventure, seeing himself as "a portion of That Might." Taking
constructive action while trusting in God would help as a vaccina-
tion to aid the dreamer "not to be puffed up, not to be gloating over
others, not to be self-centered," but to find in the swing of each
day's affairs "the oneness of Him" which might be "made manifest
in this body."

Over and over the Cayce "information" insisted on the danger
of fear and doubt, the original forces that had separated man from
God. There were indeed things for man to control within himself,

but these were not so much his appetites as his selfishness, his desire
to play God over life and his fellows with "selfish aggrandizement."
Selfishness turned natural drives into monsters, and fear and doubt
made bugaboos that need not be there. If one concentrated on the
evils to be avoided, rather than on the gifts of life, then repentance
soured into torment, as one dreamer saw in his vision where a girl,
as often for him in dreams, acted as his guide to truth.

I was anywhere at any given time. I was contemplating the
wonder of the inner power of all phenomena of the Lord. I
was reflecting upon this power's directing forms away from
the One Self—hypnotizing its portion (as Bergson puts it) so
as to appear in individual flesh form and material phenomena.
Also my experiences in this form. And I was very happy in
my double vision of the outer form and inner process.

Then a girl, seemingly representing the wisdom and consciousness of this inner power, and who seemed perfectly
aware of my limited knowledge, threw a stone into space. It
passed like a shooting star through the skies and hit some
animal there in space. "He is going to get something he
doesn't expect," said the girl, referring to me. And behold it
was so, for the stone, striking the animal in space, brought it
to earth. There were two of them and they were in cages. On
earth each crawled along on their belly like a hideous snake,
yet with head and neck upraised like powerful dragons. They
moved around, dragging their cage with them. They came
close to the girl, close to other things, and although they
looked dangerous, and I feared greatly for everything and
everyone the animals came near, they seemed to do no harm
—in fact helped matters. How I cannot say, for I felt them a
menace—i.e. viewed them with fear—but observed they did
no harm. The fear was in me, the hideous interpretation of
what I cognized, in me; but good seemed to be in them, for
they suddenly changed from hideous animals to pretty little
children, free, laughing and dancing in glee.

This pretty vision, this inspiring experience, was repeated in
this fashion: I was in a house with this girl who seemed to
represent the power, the inner impetus—the Lord of creation, or as represented in me, my subconscious self, which in
a lower dimension is present in all things. I was in the material

house and knew my elusive pretty companion was also there. Yet I had much to learn about her, and she determined to give me a lesson. Mind, now, I knew she was there, saw in the vision the lesson she planned to surprise me with—that is, I was (supposedly) unaware of her plans. I climbed up the stairs of the house, and as I did so the girl said to someone: "We'll give him a surprise and teach him." This all behind my back, so to speak. As I entered the room, instead of the beautiful girl I expected to find, I beheld a hideous black face, so ugly and so ferocious that I fainted with fright! Upon awakening I beheld the figure transformed again into the pretty girl. She stood over me, winsome, smiling and encouraging. Happy— recognizing the Spirit—I was yet afraid. 900-250

Commenting on the dream, the Cayce source spoke of "the fear" so well dramatized in the dream as "being that condition that prevents the entity from gaining the full concept, full joy, full purpose." The dreamer knew intimately his own fears—of criticism, of failure, of his passions, of pushing too hard. The answer to such blinding fears was to turn firmly away from them: "The perfect love casteth out fear. Put the love, trust and faith perfectly in Him, the Giver of all good and perfect gifts." Repentance was turning toward life, not away from evil, and such dreams could advance the prayer of the dreamer toward confession which delighted in the Lord more than it emphasized sins.

Dreams of Turning Here and Now

It was part of the Cayce picture of man that nobody need spend his time and energy justifying himself before God and his fellows. He need only turn in each action to the best that he knew; if the best were not good enough, he would be shown in his prayer life what to do further.

Oh that man would learn that lesson that good, or God, needs never . . . be justified—but glorified, in the experience of any soul! Individuals need never attempt to justify themselves for their hope, their desire, if they know the Author of that desire —as to whether it is for self, self-indulgence, self-aggrandizement, or for the glory of God and the honor of self! 2775-L-1

Part of repentance was trusting that one would be shown where to turn, where to pay attention here and now, where his prayer for strength should be directed.

An executive in a New York firm had spent a year and a half deepening his prayer life, and had begun to receive guidance almost daily, not only for his personal life, but for his business decisions. In the excitement of his new capacities, he began to seek aid in prayer almost exclusively for business achievement, rather than for his total growth. Then a dream came to beckon him to repentance.

> I entered a pawn shop and submitted my precious Sunday School medal for appraisal. The pawn shop man said, "I'll give you $800 for it." "That much?", I queried. He nodded yes—it was valuable. "Well," I commented, "I really don't altogether need it urgently, but I'll take it. I know I'll be able to pay it back real soon, so it's only a matter of form." "What name?", asked the man. "O, such and such a name," I answered, giving him a false name, for I looked at my sister-in-law and others, and wanted to hide my source of money. "You see," I justified myself, "it is only for temporary use. I am really so and so and will soon pay it back."

> He tore off half the ticket and gave it to me, but I noted he used my right name. "No," I said, "use the name—not mine." He gave me the money and motioned me away. "Well, what does it matter," I reasoned; "I'll soon pay you back." He wasn't interested. 900-132

The counseling Cayce indicated that the spiritual laws which the dreamer had studied in recent months "are for the real inner man and not of the temporal forces." What the dreamer had seen was his using spiritual laws in such a way as to become ashamed, as though he were pawning "the almost invaluable forces as are gained . . . from the study of the Word of the Creator." It was time to turn, to put first things first.

The dreamer did change. And instead of losing his business skill, he prospered. But with his prosperity came new temptations of station, as he saw in a vivid dream of Christ, two years later.

> I beheld a round sort of light of darkened hue, set rather high up. I knew it to be another consciousness, for I felt my own to be a like condition. The other said to me: "All things are

set in 'Me.' All things through Him are in 'Me.' " Then I beheld the Master, the Christ, pass in white flowing robes. He seemed to understand the needs of my understanding, much better than any of my previous [dream] interviewers, for He lifted me up and showed me exactly what this 'Me' meant. Myself, this conscious light that I felt to be me, rose up to join Him and I felt that which was in Him to be "Me." I joined Him and became consciously One with Him, such that "All things in Me" became being in "Me" myself. I felt His relationship to my consciousness, but both of us were filled with the same knowledge that composes the fully developed "Me" or "I."

Next came the application "of the knowledge," and here again the Master understood my desire for specific instances to show me how better to apply my knowledge.

We were in a Palm Beach Hotel, full of wealthy influential people. I walked down the path with some who spoke and joked of women, and I joined them. The Master passed before me and out of the gate. I should have followed Him, I know, but instead remained with these people, to whom I said: "I don't know anyone here, but I used to. I used to chase around here with Robert L.," thus trying to make an impression on my friends about my previous influential companion. Then I jumped over a ledge to join a friend of mine, and in so doing damaged some of the green leaves. A man came up and chided me, at which my friend said: "Why let him talk to you, a guest, that way?" I went up to my critic and asked him if he owned the hotel and what right he had to speak to me, a guest, in that manner. He said that he had some interest in the hotel and (as he seemed to have so many other more important guests) told me to pack up and get out. I felt humiliated. 900-315

The commentary on this dream was predictable. In the first part the dreamer had seen, said the trance-sleeping Cayce, what "was given in that message as the Master spoke; 'Seek me and I am with thee. Where I am, there ye may be also. Greater things than I do ye shall do in my name.' " The dreamer had indeed experienced the ultimate in attunement, nothing less. But later in the dream had come the choice that every man must make, "for in the vision there is experienced those vicissitudes of the worldly conditions, even in the higher social position, and the attitude of many." The dreamer would have to "choose within self the way, the manner, in which the entity would serve: whether it is better to be cast in the ways of peace from within, or to enjoy the pleasures of worldly desire for a season." What was lacking was not attunement, but application. In each day's affairs, in each social and business situation, the promise was "Speak and I will hear, for I am not afar off, but within thine own heart"; repentant prayer would help to guide application, "would man but harken to that call."

Scores of dreams were interpreted by the Cayce source as referring to sexual indulgence which needed to be curbed. Some of the dreams showed animals which needed to be kept in their place, some depicted the dreamer showing off on a stage, some used the symbolism of spots left on clothing, some presented games of spikes being placed in grooves, some showed men and women sick or alienated from one another. The problem was not in passions, as these were seen by the Cayce source, for passions correctly used in love could serve to awaken the person to his full being and relationships. The problem was where the Bible put it, in "the imagination of the heart." If one set his mind to running on passion, fed it and nurtured it chiefly on these matters, then other streams of thought were crowded out—as this dreamer saw in a dream shortly after his marriage.

> Was riding with my wife and other girls on train. A blonde and a brunette were discussing affairs, of [the kind] which I used to be familiar with, now sort of an outsider. I sort of smiled, half interestedly; as we detrained they sang in my ear some sort of song about getting children by the score. Then I went into a poolroom where four men were playing. A stout dictatorial player was showing his partner, who had a bandaged hand, how to make his shot. The man made his play and missed the pocket. "You hit the ball too low," said the stout man tersely. "How do you hit a ball if not low?" retorted the other. I left the room.

Here, said the Cayce "information," the dreamer could study how the conscious mind fed the subconscious. Whatever was whispered in the ear by one's thoughts became the material "which the subconscious digests in the sleeping or unconscious condition." The deep mind would tend to build whatever was consistently signaled to it—either a perennial and promiscuous craving, trying to make poolroom scores, or "the highest, noblest, greater thoughts." The dreamer would have to choose for himself how low he wanted to hit, where he wanted to train his imagination and creativity to run.

One could, however, indulge the imagination in knowledge as truly as in sex. A bright graduate of an Ivy League university reported this dream.

> I came to a university and sat on the steps. Someone I knew came out of the university, and pointing to his hair said, "Look how white it has turned." He then laughed and said, "You'd think I grew older in there. I'm really still young and very much alive." I noticed the white hair, yet his youth and life. 900-99

The reading suggested that "the life-giving flow" in the dreamer's existence, shown as youthful vigor, would not necessarily come "from that of the gray-haired, or premature age by concentration." Mere learning and understanding had to step outside, step off campus, and be put into "application of the understanding as has been attained." The dreamer would need to work out "the full-rounded life of the thinker," for he was becoming "lopsided" as he had seen in a previous dream that featured a beautiful oval of grass where he felt out of place.

And even if one had a balance of learning and application, there was still the necessity for simplicity of expression. A student of philosophy who was writing a book on life after death had a vivid little dream, reminiscent of Luther's visit from the devil.

> A great giant entered the door, and I threw an iron poker at him. This I repeated several times, seeking a vulnerable spot, when the poker caught in his clothing and I could not extract it. The giant advanced towards me and threatened to punch me with his big fist. He said he could blacken my eyes. He came very near to me—very, very near—about on top of me. I was afraid, yet something inside of me was not afraid. It looked bad for me, when a small girl announced a baby, and that seemed to check the giant. He withdrew, and I felt

relieved. I think it was a baby that was announced—something was—that stopped him. 900-313

From his altered state, Cayce saw the giant as criticism coming to the dreamer, for his book on the controversial topic of existence beyond death; the ridicule, especially from relatives and close associates, would seem as threatening as the dream showed. But the child and the baby in the dream represented the most helpful approach, for "the simpler the truths, and simpler the understandableness of those tenets and lessons presented," the more tempered would be the ridicule and resistance. The dreamer could find the same call to repentance from pompous expression in another area of his life, depicted in a dream from the same night.

> I was having a sword duel with my wife. She struck me on the head, splitting it open. The Voice: "Remember last October."

To interpret this dream, the entranced Cayce recalled to the dreamer an argument between the man and his wife in the previous October—and a fault of the dreamer showing then as now in his marriage. The fault? "Too many words." It was time for the dreamer to turn, to take stock of himself, for "this a continuation of that presented in the [dream of the] giant, see?"

A different man whose intent was not writing about psychic phenomena, but developing them, had this dream.

> An aeroplane rose in the sky, trying for height, and for height only. Aeroplane came to a sudden and disastrous stop. Starts its sudden crash for the earth, leaving a wake of flame from fire. . . . 137-10

The reading taken on this dream assured the seeker that he could "attain great heights in the psychic forces"—as indeed he later did by developing and using psychic capacities to secure business guidance and make himself wealthy. However, the aspiring businessman would have to keep his purpose clear, for in his vision of the plane, "the sudden descent and the blaze of fire is of the destruction that it would bring to self, if the popularity were the thought in mind." The dreamer was careful from that time on to draw no attention to his psychic efforts, but to seek, as he wrote to Cayce, "to stay in the narrow and righteous way."

Repentance was sharply signaled in a dream of a stockbroker.

> I was estimating the profits we have made, and said to an employee, who was seated at a desk, "Do you know how much money we have made?" I was thinking of the amount, and meant my partner's and my profits in our new business of the past five months. "No," he answered bluntly, "but keep it to yourself. Do not talk about it." I felt justly and rightfully rebuked, and tried to indicate that I meant not to brag, by saying, "It's income tax I mean—some tax I'll have to pay!" He stood up and smiled knowingly. "Don't talk about it," he said. I knew he was right—felt chagrined and foolish.

The rebuke had come in the dream, said the Cayce source, "that the entity may gain the more perfect understanding of self, in humbleness, in graciousness, in all those conditions necessary to make one who makes peace with their God." He who forgot to pray for humility would have it brought to his prayers by a dream.

If repentance were turning toward God with the whole heart, body, mind, and will, this did not mean that there was no "hell" to be avoided, as one philosophically inclined dreamer saw.

> I was talking to Edgar Cayce and said, "now that we know that heaven is a cosmic cognizance or consciousness . . . let us see what hell is like."

> Then I beheld a man tied diagonally to a stake. The man may have been myself. It seemed in times back, and some great king was ordering me (the man) to be burned at the stake. I (or the man) was stripped naked and the fire lighted. I suffered horribly in the flames, and then, breaking loose, I dropped on my knees to the king, a sudden idea of escape having entered my mind.

> Reaching up from my kneeling position to the standing king, I said, "You will die soon of heart disease!" He didn't believe me. I then played upon his fear or superstition. "I tell you," I ejaculated, "I am a man facing the grave, and as a dying man prophesy your death. You will die soon of heart disease!"

The king looked around wonderingly and frightened. At the same time I jumped up, and naked as I was, rushed out, making my escape.

I seemed out upon a desert or plains, and saw two or three figures coming towards me in peculiar costumes that reminded me of the "Katzenjammer Kids"—tricksters in the funny pages. Afraid that they sought some insincerity or trick, I struck one of them. 900-282

The reading assured the dreamer that he had indeed seen an experience of "the absence of that All Life-Giving Essence"—the Essence which was necessary for a person to be wholly conscious of his true relationship with God. Such an experience, of being "away from that at-oneness," was indeed what was "classified, named, called by that understanding as is called 'hell.' " But hell was not the flames, nor the torture, which merely set the stage for the dream. The true hell was not a place but a condition, a condition of separation from God which man brought on himself, by doing to another exactly what the dreamer had done to the king in the dream—playing upon fear, for his own ends. And it was, said the entranced Cayce, "fear and selfish conditions" which "first separates the entity from the presence or at-oneness with that divine Creative Energy, or God." How was the hell of separation brought about? Exactly as in the dream. He who brought fear to others found that he himself was afraid—so afraid, as to strike blindly even at comic-strip characters. For what one did to harm others became his obsession; it became the ground of his own fear, which shut him away from love as from God—until he repented.

Dreams of Turning with Others

In the view of the Cayce readings it was not enough to pray to be released from one's own panics, to be cured of one's own weaknesses. As man brought sin upon himself by turning against and away from his fellows, in selfishness, so sin was cured by turning to God with his fellows. Curing others was the key to one's own cure. As the ancient prayer put it, "Forgive as I forgive." This would be found not simply good counsel, but unyielding law.

A man given to airs over his wife reported a very simple dream, in which he heard a voice—the kind of voice which the Cayce source often described as coming from the dreamer's higher self.

> Voice: "What is the matter with my wife? That child!"
> 900-182

The Cayce trance source quickly identified the dream as a response to the dreamer's current justifications of himself in his relationships with his wife, where he was saying, "How have I not done this?" He was, as the voice had mockingly shown him, excusing himself on "those positions, stands, as have been taken." The little dream was telling him in no uncertain terms to "take stock of self and apply those laws, those lessons as have been gained within self." As the dreamer did so, he would find himself saying to his wife as had Jesus, "Neither do I condemn thee." Only as he gave up condescension to truly help his wife would he be "applying those laws as He applied in the lives of individuals who sought His counsel, His Self, His aid."

Not only in personal affairs, but in the activities of groups and institutions, repentance was to be sought with and for others. A dreamer who had once been a storekeeper reported this imagery.

> Two stores, one on Columbus Avenue carrying cheap shirtwaists, and another on Broadway, carrying a larger line of toys and stationery. The latter seemed more prosperous, but I was in the former store, whose proprietor said to me, referring to the [owner of the] Broadway store: "He thinks we could not merge to become one, but we could. I do a good business."

Then the scene changed.

> I was in a large department store, and trying to build up a business. A girl was fixing the shirtwaist counter and table. "I know where we can get some cheap shirtwaists," I said, referring to that Columbus Avenue store. 900-285

The dreamer was Jewish, and a deeply dedicated person of faith. He had often pondered how Jews and Christians could work together more closely, and in this dream, said the Cayce source, was seeing that each tradition had something to give the other.

While Christianity had the social status of the big stores, Judaism had the wares often needed. What could bring them together? Only an emphasis on service, on meeting human needs, as shown in the dream scene of trying to help the girl locate shirtwaists at a bargain. The little dream had in it the promise of an attitude of repentant helpfulness which could one day enable both Christians and Jews to "become that effervescent force, that leaven that leaveneth the whole lump." For the name of "Christian," and all the attitudes and potential idolatries and battle lines attached to it, had little meaning by itself. What was important was a process, an attitude in each individual which the term "Christlike" was meant to suggest. What was important for each person was "the position of the individual respecting its relation to the higher being, or Force, or Spirit, or All-Powerful"; institutions and names had to be made subservient to that concern in a spirit of repentance and service.

Repentance might be difficult for the pride, but one could count on the aid of "the higher forces," as one dreamer saw. A spiritual being appeared to him in a dream, and then transformed himself into the dreamer's brother, whom the dreamer needed to love and to understand—and to consult on matters as prosaic as constipation.

> Seemed I was mentally distressed over something that was wrong socially, in which I was directly concerned, particularly in my present social environment. I seemed also physically wrong, and was in bed, several channels of aid open to me—doctors, people, etc.

> But I said, "I trust and rely solely upon the Lord, my God, the ... Father; He will help me." Promptly in answer, a man walked in. Recognizing the fact that this man represented the aid I needed, and sent through the force of the Spiritual Father, I kneeled upon the bed and bowed down, face downward. The man started to talk. "You dream too much," he said. "Your dreaming might be called nefarious. Yes, that would describe your dreaming—nefarious—that is the word." Then he gave me further advice regarding social, mental, and spiritual matters, which I cannot recall.

Looking up, I saw the man change to my brother. He turned to go, and as he left, stopped and turned and was the other man who first entered. Regarding me steadily, taking my physical condition into consideration, he said, "Do not neglect to go to the toilet when you have to." Then he went out.
900-92

In the view of the Cayce source, the dreamer had indeed reached to "cosmic forces," represented by the visitor in the dream. But the service of this higher consciousness to the dreamer had not been to exalt him, but to bring him back to earth. For the dreamer was at times using his dreams and prayer experiences to draw attention from others, and to inflate himself. The dream warning of "nefarious dreaming" had been given so that he would not "be termed foolish by others, not termed as becoming a blasphemer of divine forces, or of turning same into immoral, unproper channels." It was good to dream, good to pray. But these things would avail him nothing, if he did not use them to understand and serve others—such as his own brother, into whom the dream figure had dramatically changed. While it was true that the brother's judgment of his dreaming would at times be harsh, still the dreamer needed to understand and honor his brother. If he did so, he would find the brother's counsel valuable on many things, including the moving of his bowels.

It was a dream that tempered and firmly advanced one man's prayers.

PART FOUR

How Dreams
Can Answer Prayer

CHAPTER 7

Believe the Good News: Dreams of Faith at Work

The call to "Believe the good news" which closes Jesus' compact little saying belongs with what he has already proclaimed. The good news is just the incredible nearness of the Holy One of old, imminent in the time which is fulfilled and immanent in the space closer than arm's reach. Though the Near One is too pure to behold evil, yet He beckons sinful man to turn, his evil trailing from him, to transform that same evil into glory.

But the call to believe the good news also looks away from the rest of the saying. For believing is found in acting, trusting is found in doing, assurance is found in risking.

There is a time to step out of pondering about God into His world of cars, dishes, slogans, factories, museums, prisons, beds, songs, and rockets. How is it possible to act, to act so as to believe in a Grace-ful God, and yet in the same acting fall under no spell of one's own schemes and imagination? How is it possible to distinguish *the* good news from the partial cheers and fascinations which beguile?

As a Jew, Jesus offered no private good news, no private initiation. He came of a people for whom it was meaningless to ask an individual, "Are you saved?" He spoke for a remnant which must together find favor with God, or not at all. The believing which he asked was a call for corporate response, in the common life.

To be sure, each man whom he addressed had to make his own turnings, take his own risks. But he also had a destiny to be met, to be heard, within the community of faith. As often as he cried "I believe," he was entitled to add "Help mine unbelief," and to receive aid not alone from On High, but from his fellows. As Jesus himself showed, there were dark and lonesome times, on Hills of the Skull, but it was planned for men to walk together, as they sought the belief which comes only in loving.

What, then, is the prayer of belief? Perhaps it is back to the beginning: "Our Father!" Not to a private Father, but to a shared Father. It is the prayer which allows *risking* that He has placed His mark upon every man's soul, even upon the enemy and the indifferent. It is the prayer of risking that hands can really touch, eyes meet, before the Face who gazes upon all with such even grace as shines the steady sun.

Such prayer to the one Father produces its own assurance that God hears and answers prayer. Prayer of risking leads, in its own time, to belief not easily shaken.

One person asked the entranced Cayce if there were anything in particular he could do to find and fulfill God's reason for his existence. He was told that belief grows out of work, out of doing, while it is strengthened through prayer.

> These become self-evident facts in themselves, or should, to those who apply themselves: belief in God, belief in self, belief in the divinity of man's relationship to God—accomplished for, by, and through Jesus, the Christ. The belief, the faith, the doing of what thy hands find to do which is in accord and compliance with His desires, gives purpose, accomplishes that [which is the reason for one's existence].

> For what were His words? "Father, I come to thee. I have finished." Hast thou finished the work He gave thee to do?

Hast thou sought to know the work? Hast thou walked and talked with Him oft? It is thy privilege. Will ye? 3951-MS

To be sure, finding belief through action was not, in the view of the Cayce source, a matter of forcing issues, of storming the Kingdom. All God asked of any man was that he make the effort to do the best he knew. The increase was up to Him.

> If that which confronts thee makes for discouragement, harshness of words, lack of enthusiasm ... the opportunity has turned its back—and what is the outlook? Doubt and fear!

> Study, then, to show thyself approved each day. Do what thou knowest to do, to be aright. Then leave it alone! God giveth the increase!

> For the application in self, the try, the effort, the energy expended in the proper direction is all that is required of thee. God giveth the increase! 601-MS-1

A Baptist housewife seeking to grow in her faith, in her sense of the good news, had a vivid dream which was reported to the entranced Cayce in the third person.

> She saw the face of the dying Christ, and one bleeding hand. It seemed to be a definite call to some sort of service for Him, in keeping with this particular time [wartime, 1942]. All kinds of messages then came to her, unspoken, within herself. Some were Scriptural quotations, for instance, "You have not chosen me but I have chosen you," and "Lo, I am with you always, even unto the end of the world," 540-18

Responding, the prayer-attuned Cayce sketched the necessary linkage between faith and service. The dream had been a promise.

> For, as indicated by that promise, the law of the Lord is perfect. And it ever stands as a means for an individual to become the more active to those who are so in need, from every sense, in the present.

> Thus, while the interpretation [of the dream or vision] must answer [to the dreamer] within self, this is that whereunto the entity is called: to be more active daily. Not in those ways that it would neglect any of the obligations or necessary activities about those [in the home] to whom the entity has the respon-

sibility, yet ... there is to the entity—or should be—that indication of the needs of those with whom the entity may come in contact from day to day. Let the entity, then, be up and doing with the mind and heart ... keeping with those directions that may be indicated to the entity from day to day —for, as He hath given [about directions], "I stand at the door and knock; if ye open, I will enter, and will abide with thee."

Do not be satisfied, then, with less than that, as thou hast experienced the Face, the Hands. It is with thy hands, thy manner that is expressed in thy face, that ye need to be as a daily witness for Him in these periods when many cry unto Him. Be thou, as indicated, His face to many, His hands to others, that they, too, may know the glory of the Lord in their *own* lives, their *own* experiences.

Not [asking to do] any great thing—for it is ever line upon line, precept upon precept, here a little, there a little, that is the way of the Lord. For the Law is perfect, and *converts* the soul. Thy choice, then, should be as His choice: "Thy way, O Lord, show me, day by day."

Then, enter into those administrations [of church life], those helpings to individuals as well as groups, that they, too, may take heart and give more of self in ministering to the needs of those about themselves.

These [dreams and visions], then, should be as *assurances* that He walks with thee, He talks with thee, as ye seek to do His bidding in the earth.

She asked a question. "Why have I felt within the last few years that a definite, regular period of meditation or prayer is unnecessary?" The answer was firm.

That is the spirit of wavering. ... And that experience of seeing the suffering Face, the bleeding Hand, should be that warning: be constant in prayer, meditate oft, if ye would have Him enter. This is a temptation. But forsake not thy regular period, thy daily communion, thy daily walk and talk with Him.

She asked whether the vision had been a warning of suffering coming to her, and the Cayce source responded at once that the suffering was nothing destined for her personally, but rather an indication of the suffering in others who needed her aid. Then the reading continued, explaining that service and prayer were linked.

For, as He gave, "If ye love me, feed my lambs. If ye love me, feed my sheep."

As the entity finds in its contact with individuals, daily, many have forsaken, as ye would be tempted to do, daily communion with the Christ-consciousness, daily attuning of self. [To do so is a mistake] for, as everyone ... should comprehend, God in Christ is the same, ever.

The conditions for every man's growth were the same as the conditions for Christ, and these included prayer.

Not that any individual may by [prayer] persuasion attain to having ... the Father on his side. But rather there needs to be the attuning of self to the Christ Consciousness—the oft and regular attuning of self in body, in mind, in spirit, to that oneness to which each soul may attain. For, as has been given, "Seek and ye shall find. Try me, saith the Lord, and see if I may not pour out a blessing such as ye have not even conceived!"

Thus, let the warning [in dream and vision], let that heard, be as that assurance that ye *can*—if ye will—be an emissary, be a messenger of the suffering Christ to a suffering world!

Asking a further question already touched upon in the reading, the woman inquired: "Is it important that I take a more active part in church and group work, even at the expense of my home duties and the overtaxing of my strength; or is it better for me to continue to do the things nearest me first?" She received a firm answer.

Do the things nearest thee first, but let not the greater things be left undone. Remember that warning as given Martha, because she complained that Mary neglected to do those home duties in preference to listening to the words of the Master.

What was His answer? "She hath chosen the better part."

This does not indicate neglecting home nor home duties. But the group, the church, the individuals in same, *need* that strength, that assurance which thou hast—to such a degree that thy strength will be increased as ye give out!

Remember, as He said to His disciples, "I have food, I have strength ye know not of." In giving of His strength to the woman at the well, it brought [both] that heavenly food that satisfied the soul, that makes the growth, that brings the at-onement, yea the atonement, to the soul. And this ye may have, if ye will apply thyself in the better, yea, in the broader sense.

For these [church and group] activities are thy stepping stones. Do not let them become stumbling stones.

For the way is open. His love, His wisdom, His knowledge will give thee that [which] thou hast need of daily. For the earth is the Lord's, and the fulness thereof. And the greater strength comes as ye aid others—in *their* struggle for the wisdom to apply that ability [which] they as individuals have in hand.

This also—this enabling others—enables thyself to gain the broader vision. For, as has oft been indicated here, as each soul comes into the presence of the Father, it is leaning upon the arms of someone that soul, as an individual, has attempted to assist.

Thy try? Thy purpose? Keep them in the Lord!

Ask, and ye shall receive the knowledge, the wisdom for the choice of things to do—daily. And these will bring that peace as passeth understanding.

Let thy prayer oft be—though to be sure in thine own words —to suit that period of thine own purposes: "Lord! Thou hast called unto me through thy Christ, my Savior. Here am I, Lord! Use thou me and my abilities, in the way and manner thou seest fit. Let me, O Father, be willing to use myself, my body, my mind, my purpose, to the glory of Christ, our Lord and our Savior. Help, O God, my weakness. Make me strong in thy might and thy purpose. Let me see the Light, of how I may best serve my own family, my own children, my own husband. And may I love my neighbors as myself!"

Her dream had come to anchor her prayer, and to direct and advance it. Now she would have to discover how prayer was answered with guidance and strength.

Can dreams be said to answer prayer? Can they do more than tell the dreamer what some part of him already knows? Can they bring such concrete aid that the dreamer is astonished into rediscovering his partnership with God, who allows him to risk new adventures of becoming?

The Cayce dream readings traced the helpful action of the divine in nightly dream and vision along two lines. Some dreams were interpreted as answers not to specific prayers for aid and growth but as responses to a prayerful life, kept open for needed guidance by devotional attunement. Other dreams, however, were interpreted as individual responses to the dreamer's prayers of petition and thanksgiving, aided by his receiving of the divine Self-Gift in wordless meditation.

Dreams Answering the Prayerful Life

It was the viewpoint of the Cayce trance source that the guidance and energy, as well as the transformation and growth, needed for an active and productive life, would be found flowing naturally into the consciousness, skills, and health of daily life. God did not reserve Himself for specific petitions, but constantly poured Himself upon men, when they opened the way to His aid through attunement and service. Dreams were one avenue in which answers came to each prayerful life.

The dream guidance might be as small as the glimpse of her own ridiculousness which this woman saw, as she made unreasonable demands on her husband in their daily life together.

> Dreaming, I said out loud to my husband, "Don't eat so many coats." 136-24

Or the guidance might combine health counsel with spontaneous and playful commentary on a favorite sport, as this man saw in a dream.

I saw the Columbia-Cornell football game to take place next Saturday. I saw Columbia trying to execute a forward pass. I said: "Columbia ought to win!" The Voice: "Columbia ought to win—yes—Columbia will win its last two games." Then I felt my ear [left] bother me as it does when matter flows from it 900-151

The attuned Cayce told the dreamer that the part of the dream about his ear was a warning not to go to the game, though he was a Columbia alumnus, until he had secured treatments for an old ear infection. If he did that, he could go—and he would see that his dream guidance had been correct, for Columbia would win its last two games of the season. If the lineup were not changed! (It was not, and the dreamer was confirmed.)

To some, the guidance to answer the prayerful life might come as visions of promise. A young woman dreamed these small dreams to signal the coming birth, months away, of what proved to be her exceptionally talented child.

Heard the ringing of a telephone and answered [while dreaming], saying to my husband out loud so he heard, "Don't you hear the telephone ringing? Hello!"

The Cayce comment was "A message—a message—it has come!" Her other dream accentuated her womanhood, showing gold as the promise of the birth, while her questioning was her wonder at such dream guidance, and what was "behind" it.

Saw the back yard of a building, and a woman sitting or leaning out of one of the windows. She had wonderful long golden hair. "What is back there?", I asked. 136-24

To her, as to her husband, came further dreams about the coming child, along with this little fragment for the expectant father at prayer, in mid-February.

Voice: "27th to 9th."

The Cayce source assured him that these figures represented what the man had guessed: the birth of his baby would come between March 27 and April 9. (It came April 7.) Meantime, his wife was dreaming a different kind of guidance:

> Saw Emma, the nurse I have hired for my prospective baby. In this relation I then dreamed that rich people leave their babies, but that I would (or should) stay with mine. 900-300

The unconscious Cayce assured her that the nurse was fine, but that she had much to gain, as her dream indicated, from staying close to her coming child and studying the baby's development, as part of her own study of "the subconscious" and its creative activities, in children and adults. As a well-to-do young matron, she would be tempted to turn the child over to others, but should not.

Sometimes the guidance coming in response to a prayerful life would be a warning, as this man received in a dream.

> Our chauffeur took my brother and me out in my car into the woods. He pulled up and ordered us gruffly to get out. I grew frightened at his ugly manner. . . . 137-110

The counsel of the hypnotized Cayce was simply to confirm the judgment which the dreamer himself had made, in the light of the dream and of waking experience: that the chauffeur should be released. Not so drastic a course of action was indicated in response to another little dream of stress.

> Some relationship to my brother and sister-in-law, in which I seemed trying to pull myself from the bottom of a tangle, using a rope to pull myself up. 900-255

What the dreamer was seeing, said the counseling Cayce, was a coming tangle in his relations with these relatives. He should keep his intentions upright, and the brother would in time straighten the tangle out.

But the guidance that could come in answer to a dreamer's life pattern was not automatic. There was always the need for moments of quiet attuning. By such a process, everyone could achieve the same kind of guidance that came through Cayce—as this dreamer saw.

> I saw Cayce asleep. The Voice spoke and said: "You see, there is a Christ in each and every one of us, and the Christ speaks to us from within through the law of the relativity of Force. That is how it is done." 900-211

The commentary on this dream indicated that the dreamer had glimpsed "a truth" on which he needed a great deal more study, so that he could better understand "the manner of His Spirit, dwelling within the earth's plane." There was more to it, and the rest could be found if the dreamer would "study, study, and study." As he did, dreams would continue to help his study. At the same time, he would need to keep his little daily attunements as a stockbroker, as he had seen in another dream warning him to keep his billings straight: "When the entity begins that entering of the customer's trading, enter same always with that moment of quiet, necessary to separate self from other conditions. . . ." It was counsel on momentary attunement in the midst of the day's pressures, counsel which the Cayce source never failed to offer.

The result of such turning within, even on the floor of the stock exchange, would be many kinds of guidance, including dream guidance of every aspect of business affairs. The Cayce source interpreted hundreds of dreams as dealing directly with every aspect of business: hiring and firing, forming corporations, inventions and patenting, financing, market trends, programs of selling, product design, leases, real estate, supervision, bookkeeping, advertising, office decoration, partnerships, business associates, government activities, banking trends in the United States and overseas. Not untypical was this small dream.

> Saw the names of customers on six sides of my shaving brush. Also the margin book. Voice: "Spend two afternoons a week visiting personal customers and soliciting business." 900-255

The counsel from the altered-state Cayce was to do exactly as the dream had indicated, rather than stay in the office and wait for business to arrive. Working with such dreams, two stockbrokers in particular became millionaires in their early thirties, and sailed through the Depression—which they viewed in their dreams at each stage of its course—with their holdings intact. Their dependence on prayer was seen in the counsel from Cayce a few days after the great stock crash in 1929, when he told them to take some time off: "Well that they, personally, be *out* for the next few days, that they may be able to get within themselves that stillness of purpose as comes from the constant prayer with those [forces] that would aid or guide at this time." One of the brokers took a leisurely trip to Europe not long afterward, while his Wall Street colleagues were scrambling to protect their holdings.

Through Cayce's trance aid on their dreams, not a few learned to seek dream counsel on stocks, where exact names and figures were often given for purchases and sales—alongside symbolic indications, and indications for study of particular trends. They learned to recognize familiar emblems in their dreams: trains for train stocks, cars for automotive stocks, ships for shipping stocks, a pair of rubbers for rubber stocks. Elevators and slides and crashes told them of general movements in the market, as did scores of other emblems. But often the dream material was simply literal guidance, as in this dream, which made possible a major killing in the market, by signaling that one stock would be split five for one before it was publicly announced.

> A hazy mist or cloud came before me and seemed to pass in steady movement in front of me. In the cloud or mist I saw many things, outstanding in my memory of which is the following: Pan Pet B; Havana Electric—five for one. 900-138

These men knew it was contrary to the popular stereotype of divine guidance that they could find answered prayer in business as readily as in other matters, and even their dreams reflected their doubts and fears, as this symbolic sequence showed.

> I was riding horseback and held the horse by a short rein, which when I pulled to steady the horse caused the beast to rear on his hind legs and nearly dismount me. As I gave the horse his head I seemed to ride easier—more smoothly. Then something happened; I yanked back the reins and was nearly completely thrown off, but finally managed to steady myself, and again giving the horse his head, rode on in a smoother fashion. 900-68

The entranced Cayce warned that the dreamer was seeing the indecisions in himself and his associates, with various false starts, and the temptation to claim a force that was not the dreamer's own. It was one more indication of the extraordinary difficulty of using spiritual guidance for material gain, even when that gain was used for such good purposes as hospitals and universities. But the dreamer should continue to pray and to follow his guidance—depicted in the dream, as in the "Urim" of Bible times, as coming in the form of a horse and rider. As a stockbroker, he would find people questioning him because of his money-making activity on Wall Street: "Can any good thing come from the Street? Can any force give spiritual understanding that seeks to make monies in such channels?" But the answer was firm: "The Father has chosen the weak things in life to confound the wise. Be thou wise in thy day!"

Just as dreams could guide business life, according to the Cayce source, when that life was grounded in prayer and service, dreams could and would yield health guidance. Scores of dream images were treated as referring directly to needs of the body, in diet, in exercise, in clothing, in medication, even in surgery. Every organ system of the body sooner or later turned up in the dreams submitted to Cayce, according to the interpretations given in his readings. Usually the medical dreams were simple and sensible. One man reported this dream.

> Riding on a trolley car up close to Clinton Avenue, and lost my raincoat. The trolley car ran over it. 137-24

The counsel here was that he ought to keep his body and feet dry, because he was on the edge of a cold that would be as upsetting to him as the loss of his raincoat in the dream. Another dreamer reported a train ride.

> Was riding on a train from Kansas City to New York City, and it seemed we had to come right back on the train to Kansas City again. An older man was seated opposite. He said, "Such a long trip is tiresome—one's legs ache right here"—indicating above the knees—"from sitting so long." "Yes," I concurred, and felt the pain in my legs. 900-167

The interpretation? That the dreamer needed to walk more, instead of merely sitting in his office and riding trains. But the health imagery in another little dream did not refer to the dreamer's needs, according to the Cayce trance source.

> Saw my mother rising from a couch with what seemed a pained expression, as though something hurt her. 900-166

Here, as often in health dreams, the dreamer was told he was dreaming for another, whose welfare was on his mind. He was seeing his mother's need for medical care, especially for "conditions existing in the kidney and pelvic organs, see?"

In the view of the Cayce "information," the dreams of a praying person made up a steady flow of guidance, as "answers" not alone to specific petitions, but to each day's practical needs.

Yet dreams were responsive also to specific needs, set forth in prayer and released to God's action in meditation.

Dreams and the Prayer of Emptiness

If the human drama were essentially partnership with God, as the Cayce source insisted, then maintaining that partnership, that "one-ness," was an essential business of prayer. Each person needed to pray specifically, in particular situations, his own version of "Not my will, but thy will be done." Such a prayer of emptiness—emptiness of scheming, emptiness of craving, emptiness of justification—was hard to achieve. The words might come, but the quieted state of mind and heart was sometimes difficult to find. Dreams might help to point toward it.

A businessman studying spiritual laws and psychic experiences had plunged into seeking guidance on everything he did, using divine forces even where common sense would do. Then he had the following dream.

> I was going in bathing in the ocean surf, and started to dive into a breaker, but instead found that I dived head first right into the sand, and was caught there head first. My wife called to my mother-in-law to help, and they tried to pull me out. I woke up trying to breathe, but was having great difficulty and feeling that I was suffocating from my experience in the sand. 137-84

As often in dreams, the Cayce source saw the ocean as the source of all life, as the ocean had indeed been in evolution. The dreamer was therefore depicted as plunging into his life experience, confusing "material and spiritual spheres and planes." He could use the common sense of those relatives he saw in the dream. But above all he would need to "Wade in! Don't dive in!" Then his prayer of emptiness could be as of old, "Here am I. Use me!"

An introspective dreamer who pursued his spiritual studies without including his wife saw the following dream sequence.

> Was standing in a rowboat and my wife was pulling me into land. Then they seemed to be carrying her under a shed. She seemed so like a baby, or was it a baby or not [that] they were carrying? 900-98

The Cayce source suggested that he was trying to do too much alone, forcing his own growth instead of sharing it naturally with others. In the dream, as in the story of Moses, the "drawing out of the water" of a boat and a baby was a symbol of a message—his own message that would be better and wiser if he would let his wife help him, row him. If he freed his tight grip on things and swayed with the waves, she could "be of help, succor, and aid to the body, in mind, soul, and spirit."

It was not necessary to fear either one's own conscience or God, for the prayer of emptiness could free one to work creatively with his best talents, and that was all that God required. One writer and lecturer dreamed of himself as a young lad named Tom, in a sequence which began like the parable of the Prodigal Son.

> A young boy who seemed to be a younger brother wanted money, and went in to what seemed a rather stern father to get it. The boy's name seemed to be Tom. The latter emerged from the father's room with $1.50, and went on out. Then I went in to my mother, and found her lying on a couch. She said to me, "Take care of Tom, Son, and you may have anything and everything you want." I felt a sort of emotional rush and replied timidly, "You mean that I may even have my chemistry?" "Yes, you may even have that," she replied. "I will take care of Tom," I said. (I felt like I would have anyway.)
>
> I went out and followed Tom down the street. He had built radio wires, and I noticed that it was still in process of construction. I saw the many wires stretched across like many

parallel aerials. "Into this construction I will run my individual station lines," said Tom. ... Then the whole affair
was decorated in gay fashion.

The stern father came out of the house, and looking at the
work, asked: "When was it started?" I feared his displeasure,
and interceded for Tom, saying, "He built it on his way out,
right here." I marveled at the work, as it by this time was
completely and elaborately decorated in carnival fashion. 900-
301

Using the image of radio, as it often did, to represent the sending
out of spiritual forces, the Cayce source encouraged the dreamer to
trust his own creative efforts like Tom's, which could bring good
to many, rather than to depend so heavily on approval or criticism
from others. And the way for the dreamer to defend himself from
his own threatening and punitive conscience was partly to pray
about it, plugging into the larger network, but also to help others
who stood under threat of condemnation, exactly as he had done
in the dream.

A devout man with a tendency to push his opinions on others saw
a Jewish friend making his wife sing Christian hymns, in a dream
scene.

Saw M's tall figure towering over his wife. They were singing
hymns. That is the way he made her do it. 900-116

The entranced Cayce called this dream "a figurative interpretation
of using force of any nature to succeed in bringing desires ...
physical, or of spiritual interpretations, see?" Not "force of might,"
but "that force that would be good, gentle, or that would be kind"
was what he should seek. The dream was a call to the prayer of
emptiness.

Dreams and the Prayer of Judo

As judo is the art of throwing an opponent with his own force, it
may be an image for a certain kind of prayer, where the goal of the
contest is throwing another not to his defeat but along his own life

course. The prayer of judo would be prayer to discover the true force of another person, so that one might meet him on his way, ready to hear and to help.

The Cayce readings urged seeking just such guidance. They also called attention to dreams as a source of answers to just such prayers to understand another person—friend, enemy, or stranger—for the judo of the next encounter.

A busy executive had too long ignored his mother, and had this warning dream.

> I was at some kind of affair, or in some home, with my mother and some friends. A small fire broke out, to which I paid little attention, until it grew and assumed more dangerous proportions. Then I tried to stamp it out. The floor in that spot seemed to cave in. We all became frightened and sought to extinguish the blaze. 900-253

The fire was interpreted by the Cayce source, as often in such dreams, to represent anger or temper. The "rise in temper" of the dreamer's mother had been shown, so that he could be responsive to her needs before "the results have reached those sinister conditions" of the full blaze and the cave-in of their footing together.

A man who felt himself superior to his young wife, because of his study of philosophy and psychology, had this touching dream which changed his attitude toward her, and changed his prayers from condescension to appreciation.

> Saw my wife swimming in a big bdy of water, toward the opposite shore. I noticed someone standing on a high cliff on that shore. "If she swims to there, she'll have to make the highest cliff," I remarked. She swam through the water, working hard, and I was afraid for her many times, when she seemed in danger. Finally, she arrived at the goal, and reaching out of the water, handed a silver cup to the man standing there. The man was me, and I was very happy. 900-109

As water was "the first element of life," said the Cayce source, he was seeing his wife struggling through the experiences of her own womanly life to "gain the knowledge, the place, with that one represented as being on the high cliff." It was up to the dreamer to respond to her earnest struggles, recognizing the trophy as something they could better win together than separately. What she did in her world was as brave as his elevated studying; she was worthy of his prayers and his cheers.

Edgar Cayce dreamed of a "bull with a funny head, hammer, carpet, etc." His reading told him he had seen the bullheadedness or "hardheadedness of individuals" with whom he was dealing at that time. The carpet had been an emblem of his feeling walked on, in the same relationships. But the hammer stood for the "driving force" that could prevail—not by might, but by better understanding what the hardheaded others were trying to accomplish. He would need "patience under tribulations," and would find his own judgment, "the elements of truth being from the individual self," would be confirmed, as surely as a hammer finds a nail, if he sought to be helpful rather than justified. However, wisdom was always required in judo, as another dream of Cayce's put the picture vividly.

> I was being initiated into something. There was a crowd of people around me, and they were green—like frogs standing up.

His reading told him his dream was a warning to make certain that what he offered to individuals in his work, his teaching, his conversations, was always "confromative to the use of individuals in their respective spheres." Not every vision, not every teaching of the destiny of souls, not every explanation of vibrations or psychic phenomena, would be helpful to each particular person. Indeed, if these matters were not handled with sensitivity to the needs of others, they would become "dross, as seen by that visioned in the experience," where people were made into uncomprehending frogs by ideas best reserved until they were "initiated" by their own experiences.

The prayer of judo was to understand the other person, to see his needs, his talents, his readiness. One dream made the point of judo very clearly for a financier.

> I turned in bed and beheld before me a statue in marble. It appeared as standing right next to me, or next to the bed right in the room. It was a headless statue, such as are represented in marble of the Greek God Zeus. As usual, I became fright-

ened, but I felt reassured when I reasoned that the statue was but an image or reflection of the lights that I now beheld on the ceiling. "Only an image of those lights," I reassured myself, but the statue remained, and so did the lights. 900-294

The sense of this dream was deftly noted by the Cayce source. The dreamer had seen how every man creates according to his lights. Every man built with his life his own image of God, his image of what he thought was ultimate—though he might misunderstand that Force, as the headless figure showed. Spirituality, whether in prayer or in deeds, meant meeting others by asking how they were trying to honor God, whatever their walk of life—and then helping them do it better.

A young idealist sought to raise money for the Cayce Hospital, and dreamed of others giving money for hospitals. In one such dream he was shown how he must develop his life, in order to win the confidence of donors. The dream voice said, "To get money, you must have the confidence of those who have money, that you can make money." The Cayce source confirmed his dream judgment—as well as his money-making activities, which within two years brought the full financing for the desired hospital.

To serve and grow with others, one had to understand them—and pray to understand them yet more. Dreams would answer with insight, when the prayer was the prayer of judo.

Dreams and the Prayer of Lifting

In the view of the Cayce "information," prayer and meditation were enduring resources when an individual faced a need he could not handle. In such crises, prayer and meditation lifted the divine spark within the person to a flame of unison with the One Force. In that merging, that flowing together, that answering of holy unto holy, an actual energy for change would result. From such energy might come healing for oneself and for others, as well as changes of circumstances and affairs, and the removal of seemingly hopeless burdens.

A young stockbroker, struggling to understand the prayer of lifting, dreamed the following:

> Someone (probably myself) was looking up to a corner of a tent of some kind, and the person (probably me) seemed to be ordering God. 137-31

As the Cayce source picked up the dream to interpret, it corrected the dreamer by showing him that he had in fact ordered the divine within himself, his own highest and holy self, to look up to the "High and Holy," even in the insecurity which tents represented to the dreamer. When such attunement was made, then "through the prayer of the righteous many may be saved," for real forces were always set in motion "under that direct influence of those spiritual laws."

A man much further along in his search to understand the prayer of lifting had prayed for his wife at the time of her birth of a child, and had experienced—as she had—a sense of presence and blessing which changed their lives. Asking how such healing and helping intercession worked, he dreamed of a voice which said to him'

> "The Forces need no cause of creation or reason for creative process. They are because they are, just as 2 plus 2 equals 4, and always has and always will equal 4. They do exist, and (then very loud and emphasized) *they are real!*" 900-315

Amplifying the dream, the Cayce source affirmed the reality of healing, helpful forces from God, available to every man—if man would seek them with expectancy and an open understanding.

> They are! For as given, God *is*, and they that seek Him must believe that He *is*, would they be able to become aware of that [helpful Force] He is. For when, with secular reasoning, there becomes the misunderstanding of the [Creator of even] the secular forces, there is that barrier builded over which reason stumbles, see?

The reading went on to explain why the dream had used the image of arithmetic.

> In healing, in direction [of prayer energies], there . . . are two consciousnesses to be made manifest with the one psychic or spiritual law.

In the Master—being the law—the law obeyed, rather than the Master obeying the law, for the Master *was* the law. In man this [healing activity] is as the borrowed light. For, as it has been given, "Let the light in *thee* so shine that others, seeing, may glorify That Light," see? As the Light was in Him from the reflected glory of the Father, so may the light be in *us* through His being One with the Father. The lesser light is the variation [on the One light] as heat—heat—heat, or cold—cold—cold.

For the world is the fullness of force that is of One Force, in its modified activity. ... Medicine is that necessary in the development of the individual ... to bring the healing forces. For the healing force is in the spiritual Force of Him who gave all, and not in the medicine itself—but as the agent, as the reflected light of Him who gave all.

Medicine was one way of changing the atomic structure of cells. But where did the force and pattern of those atoms originate, as well as the force and pattern in medicine? From the same One whose aid was sought and found for cells, in prayer for healing.

In the view of the Cayce source, even the effective action of medicine could be changed by the prayer of lifting—usually by meditation which raised an inward energy to harmony with the divine, for intercession. One woman saw the relation between medicine and prayer as two physicians in a dream about her mother's critical illness.

The family were quarreling over my mother and her health, and what should or should not be done. The Voice: "Listen and heed two doctors first: Dr. E—— and second Dr. ———." The name of the second doctor forgotten. 136-29

Breaking in on the dream being read to him, the entranced Cayce supplied at once the name of the forgotten doctor: "The Great Physician." He encouraged the dreamer to use the medical aid of the other physician, Dr. E——, but not to ignore the Source of all healing, who "through the spirit elements supplies that necessary for the curative forces in each and every individual." There was need both for medical skill and for earnest prayer to "the One as forgotten, One as unheeded, unheralded." The dreamer told her dream to her relatives, and they began to pray in earnest. One of them saw in a dream the action of his own prayers for the failing woman.

> At her room at the hospital. It was night and she had a new night nurse. A ray of light came from the corner of the room, growing stronger, then weaker. The ray of light continued to do that. 137-46

What the dreamer had seen, said the prayer-attuned Cayce, was the action of his own prayers as symbolized by "the new nurse" in a situation of "no hope or darkness." The light wavered as his prayers wavered, and he needed to give of himself further in the prayers. (When she recovered, the Cayce source noted that prayer had tipped the balance.)

Yet prayer of lifting was not limited to prayers for healing of the body. On the morning of his wedding day, a young man dreamed of the barriers ahead in his marriage, especially within himself.

> I dreamed I was wondering why I hadn't had visions lately, and the voice said, "Pay close attention to this dream of veils." Then I was selecting veilings in a store, most black in color, and selected six from a number, to cover the face. I said, "I don't understand that dream, but my Father in Heaven will explain it to me." The voice answered, "The veils are the conditions of your better understanding, your advancement."

The Cayce trance source would not describe for the dreamer his veils, except to confirm that the description of the voice in the dream was correct. The young man would have to turn to the Father in prayer, to find those veils, and to discover how to lift them. The dreamer took the counsel seriously, as his later dreams showed. But the barriers were many, and in a few years he and his wife were divorced. His dreams showed him that at least some of the veils had been found and dealt with, some of what the Cayce reading had indicated at the start of the marriage, when the veils were called what must be "laid aside or changed," as his life was "covered" not by man but by God, who in His time would over-shadow a devout man's sins and weaknesses.

Dreams and the Prayer of Dancing

Not all prayer, in the perspective of the Cayce "information," was prayer for critical needs, or prayer of solemn penitence. Indeed, the spirit of most prayer ought to be a spirit of joy.

The prayer group that formed in response to a dream by Cayce took a phrase from a reading on prayer and meditation and put it at the head of their prayer list: "He that would know the way must be oft in prayer, joyous prayer."

Such prayer might not, however, be easy to conceive. Dreams could help to quicken the spirit of joy. For the full life of prayer, the full Good News of the Kingdom, included a prayer of the dance —a spirit of celebration before the Lord. When this dancing was gone, dreams could help to restore it to the one who prayed.

Edgar Cayce found his spirits low in 1933, after losing the Cayce Hospital and Atlantic University, the hopes of his lifetime, when the Depression brought strains that divided and ultimately removed the backers of each institution. He wondered aloud what good could be found in his peculiar gift. Then he dreamed a little dream that set his perspective straight.

> Dream had some time ago, regarding a baby that was very remarkable, talking before an audience that was spellbound. It was being examined to see that it wasn't just a midget, and no one could find fault. All agreed it was a prodigy.

The reading taken on the dream explained that the child in the dream had represented his own gift, seeming to Cayce himself to be "little, or of no purpose in the present, and in its environ." But as a child grows, so could the helpfulness of the gift yet grow "to make the hearts, souls of men, of that turn which brings Life itself." Nothing less than surprised delight over a talking baby was appropriate as the spirit for Cayce's work and prayers, even in a dark time. He needed the prayer of the dance.

A young husband whose wife was pregnant reported an unexpected dream.

> Dreamed that my wife gave birth to one—to twins—to triplets; to one, two, three. 900-183

Rather than foreseeing the actual outcome of the birth, said the Cayce source, the dreamer had viewed an emblem of the creative process itself, where one and one makes three—just as parents produce a child. When the life of a man and the life of a woman were fully joined, "in physical, mental, spiritual balance," the result was always more than their individual efforts. God Himself sent His blessings as fruit of their labor. Not only in childbirth, but in all their doings, they should rejoice at what they could bring about together—and pray that way "in the full union of two minds."

This was a spirit of dancing.

The friction between a sales executive and his sister-in-law brought forth a mischievous dream to quicken the spirit of the dance in their lives.

> Seemed to be in a modest apartment such as we used to live in. I was trying to please my sister-in-law, by cutting up with her, so to speak. In a peculiar position, I tried to take her picture with her husband's movie camera. It was a hard position (physically) to assume, and I found I could not take her picture anyway, because there was no film in the camera. However, I thought, it didn't matter because it was all in fun; I was trying to please and amuse her. 900-232

The reading encouraged the fun and teasing as the best way to the reconciliation for which the dreamer had prayed. Good humor and even ridiculous postures could put him in her "good graces." He need not sacrifice his principles, but only apply the "same lesson as has been given of old: 'I will be all things unto all men, that I may thereby save the more'—see?"

In corporate affairs as in personal affairs there was a spirit of dancing, a spirit of mutual delight and respect, which could make all things new. Cayce himself was explaining to a friend one morning his understanding of the differences between denominations. Then, while he was giving a reading, he had a dream that carried forward the thought. He reported it as he awakened.

> Now, for instance, consider a field of corn. In the grain of corn there is life. Man plants it in the soil, works it, and then he reaps the harvest. Not every man selects the same kind of corn. Not every man ploughs it alike. Not every man sows it

alike. Yet in each case it brings forth the very best it is. It is the God or the Life within each grain that the man is seeking. It sustains his body, and also produces enough seed to raise more. That's religion. That's the denominations.

The prayer of the dance was the prayer of delight in diversity. It was the prayer that caught the essence of the Creative Forces at work.

One dreamer who had prayed and struggled long—and at last successfully—with his drives toward girls had a dream which used the imagery of no less than girls, to set before him the promise of the Kingdom of God.

> Saw a chorus of girls dancing on stage. One at a time the girls would come to the front and each do an individual dance. 900-114

To Cayce in his prayer-induced trance state, the imagery of this dream, unlike that of many of the dreamer's previous scenes, was "a physical action giving ... lessons in spiritual thought." Each person in the world, as the dreamer could see, had his part to play, his lesson to share, when his turn in the line came for his own original expression—"meaning again, service—service—service." This was the Kingdom of God, the Reign of the Present One, found in the fullness of time wherever it was accepted—starting with the next chorus line, or the next dream.